*"This book should be in the library of every pastor and elder who wants
to make their areas of influence a better place in which to live and work in
anticipation of Jesus' soon return. The wisdom that Pastor Arrais has gained
over the years clearly shines through in this book."*

MATTHEW BEDIAKO, SECRETARY,
GENERAL CONFERENCE OF SEVENTH-DAY ADVENTISTS

*"Jonas Arrais has made a valuable contribution to the literature for ministry
with this book. The need for growing and mature Christians in a negative world
is self-evident. Leaders will find his scriptural approach to life-long growth
and learning a valuable addition to their reading material."*

GERRY KARST, GENERAL VICE PRESIDENT,
GENERAL CONFERENCE OF SEVENTH-DAY ADVENTISTS

*"This comfortable read provides a vision of how God's people
in local church settings can achieve harmony and sustain unity
while facing a challenging future in a turbulent world. It makes a great
'book club' selection for an entire congregation or for small groups."*

ELLA SIMMONS, GENERAL VICE PRESIDENT,
GENERAL CONFERENCE OF SEVENTH-DAY ADVENTISTS

"Jonas Arrais has a message that all church members, in whatever position, ought to listen to. It's a very practical guide, well written and well thought out, regarding the daily life of the church. Reading the book is one thing; we need the courage to implement what it teaches."

CLIFFORD GOLDSTEIN, DIRECTOR,
ADULT SABBATH SCHOOL BIBLE STUDY GUIDE,
GENERAL CONFERENCE OF SEVENTH-DAY ADVENTISTS

"Jonas Arrais has compacted in this volume a significant array of church leadership principles that will significantly enrich those involved in leading the people of God. This book is a must-read for leaders in local congregations."

ANGEL MANUEL RODRIGUEZ, DIRECTOR,
BIBLICAL RESEARCH INSTITUTE,
GENERAL CONFERENCE OF SEVENTH-DAY ADVENTISTS

"There is a profound—perhaps eternal—difference between 'playing' church and being the church. In this insightful, fast-paced book, Pastor Jonas Arrais demonstrates the need for authentic Christian ministry, loving Christian leadership and the resulting dynamic Christian community that the world longs to see. Read these pages to find a road map to a successful, growing church!"

MARK A. KELLNER, NEWS EDITOR,
ADVENTIST REVIEW AND *ADVENTIST WORLD* MAGAZINES,
SILVER SPRING, MARYLAND

"The author of this book is an experienced pastor and trainer of church leaders. As you look for material that will make you more effective, this book will help awaken your creative thought."

NIKOLAUS SATELMAJER, EDITOR, *MINISTRY*

A
P+SITIVE
CHURCH
IN A NEGATIVE
W-RLD

*Learning and Improving
Leadership in Every
Experience of
Your Church*

JONAS ARRAIS

Published by
Ministerial Association Resource Center
General Conference of Seventh-day Adventists
12501 Old Columbia Pike
Silver Spring, Maryland 20904 USA
(301) 680-6502
www.ministerialassociation.com

This book was
Designed by Ron J. Pride
Cover art by SW Productions
Typeset: Bembo 11/13

Bible texts in this book marked NIV are from the Holy Bible, New International Version. Copyright © 1973, 1978, 1984, International Bible Society. Used by permission of Zondervan Bible Publishers.

PRINTED IN U.S.A.

ISBN 1-57847-047-1

Special thanks for Developmental Funding:

J.A. Thomas & Associates
Hospital and Physician Consulting

DEDICATION

To my spouse
Raquel Costa Arrais
My best friend and love for 25 years.

and

To my sons
Tiago Costa Arrais
Andre Costa Arrais
Who motivate me to face the future with confidence.

ACKNOWLEDGMENTS

*To the General Conference Ministerial Association
for providing support to write this book.*

CONTENTS

Foreword 11

Introduction 13

1. Creative Changes are Healthy 15

2. Creative Changes are Needed 23

3. Decision–making 28

4. The Danger of Negativity 32

5. Applying Biblical Principles 38

6. The Challenge of Change 46

7. Maintain Christian Ethics...................................51

8. Ethics in Control 59

9. Biblical Discipline 65

10. The Importance of Conviction and Confidentiality 72

11. A Mature Approach to Discipline 79

12. Doing What is Right in the Right Way................85

13. Your Good Name is Safe in our Home 93

FOREWORD

One of the many things which can concern a church leader—and should—is the sight of members, new and old, departing via the "back door" while new converts come in the front.

There are many reasons why people leave church, but the lack of a positive, nurturing atmosphere is probably high on the list. People come to church not only to worship the Lord, they come to feel part of a spiritual and loving family.

It's a tough world "out there," and, as my colleague, Pastor Jonas Arrais points out, it's a very negative one. If you don't believe me, put this book down for just a minute and flip on CNN—you'll see plenty of negative news there, I assure you!

The church should not be—indeed it must not be—a place where the negative is allowed free reign. Instead, the church must be a place where the weary saint can find rest and restoration—a positive oasis in this negative world. Jonas Arrais understands this as only one who has served "in the trenches" can fully comprehend.

Jonas Arrais, along with his spouse and ministry partner, Raquel, has pastored major congregations in huge cities and mentored hundreds of fellow pastors and laity leaders in how to build a church with a positive atmosphere.

He has observed the crippling effects of strife, gossip and, most tragically, church discipline gone wrong. Restoration is reduced, fellowship is fragmented, and lives hang in the balance when a church reflects the super-competitive, uncaring spirit of the world in which we live.

There is a way out, however, and Jonas shows it to us from the Bible and also from the counsel of Ellen White. He demonstrates that offering a positive focus, even in the worst situations, opens the door to healing, restoration, and even to heaven itself for those in deepest need—our wounded saints.

I want to experience a church that helps those who are suffering and which is committed to preserving the good name of their fellow members and to helping heal those who are wounded. So does Jonas Arrais. And so will you after you finish this compact, compelling volume.

Read it, re-read it, and implement its steps. The fellowship you save may truly, indeed, be your own!

James A. Cress
Silver Spring, Maryland, United States
September 2007

INTRODUCTION

"Do not forsake wisdom, and she will protect you; love her,
and she will watch over you"
—Proverbs 4:6, NIV

When Solomon asked for wisdom so that he could lead God's people with skill and discernment, the Bible says that his request pleased God. In answer, God gave him not only what he had requested, but much more than he could ever imagine (I Kings 3). Today, God still rejoices when His followers seek knowledge to use in leading His people.

In the prophet Jeremiah's days, Israel was in intense apostasy. The people had turned away from God, partly due to their leaders' spiritual frailty. God made a promise to the prophet with the purpose of reviving the spiritual lives of His children: "Then I will give you shepherds after my own heart, who will lead you with knowledge and understanding" (Jeremiah 3:15, NIV). Today, God is still seeking spiritual leaders who are able to lead His people with knowledge and understanding.

This book was written for church leaders who believe in a creative God; For those who believe in a God who communicates wisdom and who empowers His children to do their best for His church; for those who believe you can grow and learn much more about church leadership; for you who are wise and want to be wiser. The Bible affirms this truth: "Give instruction to a wise man, and he will be still wiser" (Proverbs 9:9, NKJ).

All leaders should recognize that when they stop growing, they reduce their potential for service. Therefore, never stop growing, or you will be like yesterday's bread—dry and moldy (Joshua 9:5). Rick Warren says, "The moment you stop learning, you stop leading, and your organization stops growing." Similarly, Thomas Edison said, "Show me a thoroughly satisfied man and I will show you a failure." It is essential for all of us to develop a lifelong love of learning coupled with humility that will make us yearn to become better leaders

This book, *A Positive Church in a Negative World,* can help you broaden your horizons with practical vision. You can help transform the negativity that may exist in the church today and encourage a more positive and healthy experience.

These chapters will challenge you to view some traditional procedures within your church with a wider, more balanced, and creative vision. You will also reflect upon common mistakes that we may make as spiritual leaders and you will certainly be led to abandon some old concepts and traditions which you may have followed for many years. Your desire to change for the better will increase. Your great goal will become to venture into new paths. You will discover new concepts of what it means to lead God's church well.

Of course, this book – like many others written about church leadership – has limitations. Its intention is not to provide solutions for every problem which the church might face, but to help us eliminate some harmful concepts even as we stir a creative, renewing spirit within our souls.

As you dream and work for a better and more positive church, don't be tempted to make comparisons or ask, "'Why were the old days better than these?' It will no longer be wise to ask this kind of question" (Ecclesiastes 7:10, NIV).

In this book, I try to share experiences from my personal pastoral ministry, presenting some concepts which life has taught me combined with others which I sought through study, reflection, and communion with God. I hope this book will become a blessing in your life and for your church. Although our world may be growing worse every day, I believe that we can improve our church to make a positive impact in a negative world.

Spiritual Leadership is like a plane trip: after each segment of the flight, the plane must stop to refuel. I hope this book becomes a refreshing stop for your spiritual refueling. May Jesus' words remain with you: "'Come aside by yourselves to a deserted place and rest a while.' For there were many coming and going, and they did not even have time to eat" (Mark 6:31, NKJ).

Best wishes for good reading, blessings in your personal life, and success in your spiritual leadership!

Jonas Arrais

1

CREATIVE CHANGES ARE HEALTHY

"See things as you would have them be instead of as they are."
—*Robert Collier*

Why is creativity so important? Are we all creative? Are leaders born with this trait, or is it acquired? Can creativity be cultivated and encouraged? What is creativity, after all? And why is creativity important for people involved in church work?

Myron Rush mentions two benefits of creativity: (1) It can solve administrative problems; (2) It helps us find new and more effective ways to do the job.[1] In church administration, it is possible to improve many of our activities, programs, and tasks by employing creativity. When church leaders value creativity in carrying out their responsibilities, they will often discover more practical and wiser solutions for many problems.

DEFINING CREATIVITY

A creative person sees the same problem as everybody else, but innovators think of new options and different solutions. I define creativity as the act of turning new and imaginative ideas into reality.

Creativity also involves two processes: thinking and producing. Innovation is the production or implementation of an idea. If you have ideas but don't act on them, you are imaginative but not creative.

We can learn to see any subject from a new and different perspective. The urgent need in our day is the ability to look at a question in a new way and to see what no one has seen before. Creativity allows us to grasp new ideas and preexisting concepts and to form new tactics or

15

structures that will solve a common problem in an uncommon manner. Creativity may also produce ideas that are very different from the way we've "always done it."[2]

Thus, creativity is the ability to do something new, to view an idea in a new way, or to give new form to that which already exists.

DEVELOPING CREATIVITY

In mid-15th Century Germany, a goldsmith named Johannes Gutenberg designed movable type. At first his idea was considered madness, but he persevered. The first book of great importance produced by his printing press was the Bible in Latin. Printed copies began to compete with the most beautiful handwritten manuscripts. By 1500, this new method had been used to print Bibles in six languages—German, Italian, French, Czech, Dutch, and Catalan—and by the mid-16th Century in eight more languages—Spanish, Danish, English, Swedish, Hungarian, Icelandic, Polish, and Finnish.

Enabling people to read the Scriptures in their own languages was a pioneer project. Gutenberg looked beyond the way things had always been done to create a truly earth-changing innovation.

Here's good news! Creativity is a part of human nature and it can be developed. Horácio Soares, in his article "Desenvolvendo a criatividade"[3] ["Developing Creativity"], describes several important steps to help improve our creativity:

• **Take notes.**

Ideas are like dreams. If good ideas are not properly addressed, they will be forgotten and lost within a few minutes. Therefore, write down any and every idea, even those that may make no sense. Preserve even those ideas which seem immature or have not yet awakened the interest of anyone else. Write it down! "When Einstein was asked the location of his laboratory, he took a pen and answered: 'Here!'"[4] Take notes!

• **Develop curiosity.**

Curiosity is one of the most important fuels for creativity. Developing curiosity can overcome apparently impossible challenges. Creative individuals use their boundless curiosity to gather information about a problem and to seek better solutions. Einstein said, "I have no special talent, only that I am passionately curious."

• **Write down at least one idea each day.**

This is a simple exercise that, if done on a regular basis, will bring interesting results in a short time. Do the following every day. Spare a few minutes—during your shower, commuting to church, before going to bed, or during any other activity—to contemplate a specific subject. Think about new solutions for old problems. Contemplate ideas for new prob-lems. Ponder answers for difficult questions you face. Try this exercise daily and write down and store every idea that may come to you.

> "Man's mind, once stretched by a new idea, never regains its original dimensions."
>
> —*Oliver Wendell Holmes*

• **Store your ideas.**

Some ideas need to rest in order to mature and gain new life. Many times, today's idea may solve tomorrow's problems; therefore, write down and store all your ideas.

A good tip to avoid forgetting your ideas is to buy a note pad, preferably a journal with a hard cover, to record any ideas or thoughts that may occur to you. You cannot select the time or place for good ideas to occur. If you don't write them down quickly, you will certainly forget them.

• **Learn to hear, listen, and observe.**

People, places, facts, and circumstances may awaken within us answers and ideas at any time. We must learn to codify these messages through our own experience, perception, and intuition. Use all means and senses in search of the best answer for what you need.

Psychologist Samuel Gosling stated that we need to notice small de-tails in order to develop a full vision about a person or a problem. Certain particulars or details may awaken comprehension of the overall challenge.

• **Pay more attention to children and the elderly**

Picasso declared, "Every child is an artist. The problem is how to re-main an artist once he grows up." The most creative ideas are usually the most obvious and simple ones. Children are the essence of simplicity and we can learn much from observing their play activities and listening to the stories they invent.

On the other hand, we have the elderly, with all their experience and wisdom accumulated through much hard work. If we observe other cul-tures we can learn the value of respecting these very special people who have a lot to teach us.

If we put together the simplicity of children and the experience of the elderly, we'll have a powerful source of ideas.

• Understand first; judge later

Bias is a dangerous obstacle to creativity. Do not judge what is unfamiliar and different. It is important to keep your mind open for changes, newness, and diversity that may come up. The best ideas may come from the differences among people, things and ideas.

• Learn to enjoy problems

A problem is always a challenge, but it can be a great opportunity to create and innovate. We need to learn to appreciate problems and challenges that may come our way. Optimists see opportunities in every problem. Pessimists see problems in every opportunity.

• Do not fear questioning

The fear of asking a senseless question and looking silly and incompetent before strangers, co-workers, or friends makes us feel insecure. We may lack the courage needed to clarify our doubts.

To have the courage to ask, question, and doubt is the way to better understand the problem and to take the first step towards a creative solution. One of the childlike characteristics present in creative adults is the ability to ask questions about subjects that, in general, are no longer questioned by adults.

> "He who exchanges bread, keeps only one. He who exchanges ideas keeps both. The best business is exchanging ideas."
>
> —*Machado de Assis*

• Put your ideas into action

To have ideas is not enough; we need the courage to demonstrate them. When we present an idea, it grows, it is transformed, and it reaches another sphere. It is then that we can test it and visualize its real possibilities.

We need the courage to try, even knowing that we will probably suffer many falls along the way. We should never forget that the worst ideas are always the ones that never came out of the drawer.

• Maintain good humor

Edward de Bono suggests that, "Humor is by far the most significant activity of the human brain." Robert Menna Barreto says, in his book *Criatividade no Trabalho e na Vida* (*Creativity at Work and in Life*),

18

that there are some ingredients which we need in order to have creative ideas. Good humor is one of those. It helps us to face problems.

While I was finishing this chapter I had some personal problems that took away my jovial spirit and power of concentration. As a result, I couldn't write a line for almost an entire week.

It is very hard, I would say almost impossible, to maintain a good attitude when we are facing a personal problem that makes us sad, discouraged, and hopeless. But even then we need to raise our heads, face the problem, and walk through it. When I regained a more pleasant disposition, I began to see the problem from a different perspective and discovered it wasn't as ugly as it seemed.

• **Work hard**

"I think ninety-nine times, and I can't discover anything; I stop thinking and plunge into silence; here is when truth is revealed to me." – Einstein.

Einstein's discoveries were the result of much dedication and work. Plunge your head into the problem, study it in depth, and look for the greatest number of possible answers. Like Einstein, after working hard, detach yourself a little from the problem and when you least expect it, you'll probably find the answer you sought so much.

YOU CAN BE CREATIVE

It is believed that the human creative potential has its beginning in childhood. When children's creative initiatives are complimented and stimulated by the parents, children tend to become bold adults, prone to act in an innovative way. The opposite also seems to be true.

"Psychologists studying creativity have discovered that it is based on cognitive processes we all share. Creativity is not the result of some magic brain region that some people have and others don't."[5] We all have the ability to do something new or to reformulate what already exists. Human beings' creative potential is almost unlimited.

To Abraham Maslow, one of the most prominent psychologists of the 20th Century, "A creative man is not a common man to whom something was added. A creative man is someone from whom nothing was taken." Creativity is not a gift or a talent that only a few privileged ones receive. No one needs to take a continuing education class to become creative. No extraordinary effort is needed either. Such ability is the natural result of the human thinking process.

When God promised the prophet Jeremiah that He would give spiritual leaders to lead His people, the Lord presented two qualities besides spirituality that are fundamental for a creative and innovative leadership: knowledge and understanding (Jeremiah 3:15).

THE CREATIVE PROCESS

During the creative process, certain stages are often observed:

• **Problem perception.** This is the first step in the creative process, and it involves recognizing the problem or challenge.

• **Problem theorization.** After observing the problem, the next step is to convert it into a theoretical or mental model. When we face any problem, we start collecting as much information as possible. After collecting data, we think about the problem based on the information we have. We need to read, discuss, take notes, collect information, and focus our attention on the subject. We need to ponder the question and live with it day and night while our ten billion neurons are warmed up to answer the critical question: What should I do to solve this problem?

"You are doing your best only when you are trying to improve what you are doing."

—*Anonymous*

• **Consider/see a solution.** This step generally begins by a sudden glimpse of the solution; it is the moment solutions suddenly appear. It is when we are able to visualize the solution to the problem. It is Archimedes' classic "EUREKA!" Many of these moments come only after an exhaustive study of the problem.

• **Producing the solution.** The last stage is to convert the mental idea into a practical one. It is considered the most difficult stage, often described as "1% inspiration and 99% perspiration."[4]

CREATIVITY IN A PARABLE

The parable of the talents contains several biblical principles of management and leadership. When Jesus told this parable He wanted, among other things, to teach that every Christian should make good use of his or her talents and creativity. The servants who decided to risk, invest, and put their creativity to work multiplied their talents. On the other hand, the servant who felt intimidated by the challenge and did not believe in his creative potential disappointed his master (Matthew 25).

OUR GOD IS CREATIVE

That is how God is: creative, dynamic, and wonderfully innovative. There are no two people created alike. This is the way God works. We also can innovate to create new forms of evangelism, of praise, and new ways to worship the Lord. We innovate in order to bring more people to God.

God is the source of everything that is good (James 1:17). He is goodness in its essence. When God created all things, He not only saw that everything He created was good, but He acknowledged the glory of His creativity as well.

Being a disciple is living with a creative God who makes something new every day. God's creativity is amazing. Have you ever stopped to think about the great variety of animals, fish, birds, and plants? Man has yet to discover some of them! And if we stop to think that on a giant planet such as ours, no two people are alike, it seems almost incredible! He was careful to think creatively about details that would make all the difference. Have you ever seen two identical sea shells on the beach?

The Bible declares, "See, I am doing a new thing! Now it springs up; do you not perceive it? I am making a way in the desert and streams in the wasteland" (Isaiah 43:19).

God is saying through the prophet that this is the time for transformation, and He affirms with enthusiasm, "I am doing a new work here! It is springing up. Can you have a glimpse? Can you see it?"

Give up on what is unnecessary; change your opinion if need be. Learn more, study what you don't know, and be humble enough to accept good counsel. No matter what God asks of you, obey Him. When you do that, you will begin to see roads opening up in your desert.

May your prayer be, "Dear Father, keep on doing Your work in my life and help me to see quickly what you are doing, that I may seek to understand and co-operate with you."

In the next pages you will find more concepts and ideas that will help you to recognize and understand the importance of creativity in the context of church leadership.

[1] Myron Rush, *Management: A Biblical Approach*, pp. 24-25 (Victor Books, 2002).

[2] Margaret A. Boden, "What is creativity?" in *Dimensions of Creativity*, M. A. Boden, ed. (MIT Press, 1994).

[3] Horácio Soares is a university professor in Candido Mendes in Brazil (ESCM). Article published on the Internet, internativa.com.br/artigo_criatividade.html

[4] Humberto Rohden, *Einstein – O Enigma do Universo*.(Martin Claret Books, 1989)

[5] Neil Schoenherr, "You Too Can Be Creative; It Just Takes Hard Work" Washington University in St. Louis - News & Information, (February 2, 2006).

[6] Myron Rush, *Management: A Biblical Approach*, pp. 24-25 (Victor Books, 2002).

2

CREATIVE CHANGES ARE NEEDED

*"Discovery consists in seeing what everyone else has seen
and thinking what no one else has thought."*
-Albert Szent-Gyorgyi

Early in my pastoral ministry, I recognized the value of creativity. Since then I have tried to see my various ministerial responsibilities from this perspective. In this book I will share a story that took place in my ministry. I will examine various aspects of the story in each chapter, presenting church leadership applications that can help local pastors and church leaders become more effective as they plan church activities.

One day a member of my congregation came to me with a seemingly naïve question. Simply and directly he asked, "Pastor, in order for me to be a church officer does my name need to be approved by the church committee?" I quickly answered, "yes," and I tried to explain, saying that his name really had to be considered by the nominating committee before he could exercise any ecclesiastical function. I also explained that the final step in his approval would be a vote by the congregation.

Quickly, he made the following request, "Then, pastor, please do not nominate me for any position."

I confess I was really intrigued by that request. Was he implying that he was disappointed by the way the church or the pastor worked?

My first reaction was to clarify his response. I asked him what he meant, for it seemed as if he didn't trust my leadership or the work of the church committee members. He responded in a good spirit revealing honestly, "The problem is that when a name goes to the church nominating committee, more negative than positive comments are made about that person. I would like to preserve my good name in the church. Please, pastor, do not nominate me for anything."

> "Be the change you want to see in the world."
>
> —Mahatma Gandhi

I felt very uncomfortable with his observation. After all, I was the church pastor and president of the church committee. If something wasn't functioning properly as the pastor I was responsible.

When we meet problems we may respond in various ways. They may either encourage us to keep on going or paralyze us. We may interpret them as an excuse for failure or as steps to success.

CHALLENGES GENERATE OPPORTUNITIES

Certain problems and challenges that come up in the church may be signs that changes are needed. Sometimes we have a hard time detecting these needs, for often the signs come up at the most unexpected or inappropriate times. Furthermore, the people involved may bring with them or cause resentment, anger, grief, and disillusion.

That conversation led me to a deep reflection about the way we often behave when we lead a church. It was not easy to digest a comment of that nature. But, little by little, I began to admit that he was correct in his observation.

Many scenes of church committee meetings and other church activities began to replay through my mind like a movie. I confess that I felt God was trying to tell me something through that conversation. It is important not lose the ability to hear God's voice speaking to us through His people or by means of simple experiences that He allows.

I began to realize that preserving the name and reputation of each member of the family of God is part of the pastoral ministry, as well as that of the spiritual leaders' and members' ministry. Unfortunately, in many churches care and respect may not be shown. When it is our own name that is the target of comments we expect Christian ethics to be practiced, but many times we are not nearly as careful when we are discussing someone else's.

After reflecting upon the way the church had been acting I concluded that this brother was correct in his observation and concern. Something really needed to be changed in the way I led my church. As a pastor my courage, sensitivity, and creativity were needed to improve the situation.

Some of the hurtful practices that exist in the church are like weeds that appeared over time and became almost a natural part of church life. This usually happens because at some point the appropriate person didn't act or make the correct decision.

When action is needed but no decision is made conditions begin to deteriorate. The problem may be that some leaders avoid risks. They do not understand that part of their ministry involves a possibility of failure.

On the other hand, sometimes as products of a Christian culture we easily accept what has been practiced for generations. We don't stop to evaluate certain practices and procedures. We may do things as they have always been done without allowing for, or even encouraging innovation, creativity, and change.

A leader needs to respect traditions, but he must also have a greater respect for people. If a tradition is valid and useful, a leader may use it to reach important goals. However, an efficient leader should question useless or harmful traditions, or traditions that impose unnecessary burdens upon people. "We've-always-done-it-that-way" is not a good rationale for a leader; instead, the good leader asks, "Why?" and "Can we do better?" When convinced that a new way is an improvement, the creative leader works to bring about that change.

On the other hand, when breaking traditions, it is imperative to take the time to build support and to explain the new ideas to church members in a clear way that they may understand.

EVALUATE REALITY

It is wise for spiritual leaders to reflect and evaluate honestly how we are conducting the ministries of our church. We need to ask ourselves, "What factors are not promoting the members' unity and well being? What are we doing that should be improved?" When we ask these important questions we can find the answers to some of the problems affecting our church, our Christian community.

When realistically evaluating our church to identify mistakes we make as leaders, we need to be sensitive to the signals members are giving us. Often they provide good clues that something is not going well. If we are really brave, we can even use well-constructed surveys to help pinpoint significant concerns.

Once I read a story that illustrates the need for member feedback. An airplane was ready for departure. The passengers were settled in their seats. However, the pilots had not yet arrived. The co-pilot arrived very late, yet very calm. Wearing dark glasses and holding a cane, he tried to find the control cabin. The passengers were frightened, for they saw the co-pilot was blind. While they discussed what they should do, the pilot arrived. He was also wearing dark glasses and was being lead to the control cabin by a guide dog. The passengers could not believe their eyes. While they considered leaving the aircraft, the doors were closed, and the plane began to move towards the take-off runway. The frightened passengers tightened their seat belts even more. The plane began to gain speed. It went faster and faster, but didn't take off. The nervous passengers could see from the windows that the airport was far behind and that they were getting to the end of the runway. When they saw the plane was going to hit the wall at the end of the runway, they all screamed together, "It's going to crash!" At that instant the plane took off. The pilot then commented to his blind colleague, "Man! Today it took them a while to scream!"

The signal for those two blind pilots to take off was the scream of the passengers. Unfortunately, sometimes the same thing happens at church when members are concerned about certain problems or they are dissatisfied about matters such as visitation, preaching, reverence, relationships, worship quality, and other topics. Even in the face of negative comments from a dissatisfied congregation pleading for something better and for creative changes, many leaders do not take off in their ministry.

> "God makes three requests of His children: do the best you can, where you are, with what you have, now."
>
> —*African-American proverb*

All of us can use our creativity and ability to innovate or improve present methods. That is why the leader who wishes to move forward should pay attention to the signals from members and to the good ideas they suggest.

My conversation with my church member who preferred not to be nominated could have been just one more of many that take place in the church hallway, but it wasn't. In moments like these we may either open or close the door to improving our ministry. Every leader knows that success, in part, depends upon their ability to make right decisions. Just as wrong actions may bring serious consequences, correct ones may produce great rewards. One thing is certain: we'll always have the opportunity to respond positively. Every time we decide to answer in a positive and creative way, we'll be doing ourselves a tremendous benefit and can make a significant difference.

THERE IS ALWAYS A BETTER WAY

When we do not reflect on and evaluate our methods, we run the risk of repeating the same mistakes made in the past. We can develop a ministry that is stuck in a rut. Some leaders today follow the same path and proceed the same way as past leaders, never questioning whether earlier leaders, methods, and plans were the best. As a result, we often do not visualize nor experiment with other and better alternatives.

Leaders who do not occasionally stop to evaluate and consider new ideas will lose the great opportunity they were given to make a difference. They will probably be remembered, if remembered at all, as having been just one more leader who served the church in the old way.

Life is a school where every day we have the opportunity to learn or unlearn. Looking back, I feel a little sad, because I see that many of the mistakes I made in my ministry were due to lack of instruction, vision, creativity, evaluation, and reflection. But each of us comes to a moment when we have the opportunity to make a decision: we can persist on the same way or seek a better way. A bold decision may move us from the path of normality and mediocrity to the highway of creativity and of a ministry that really makes a difference.

3

DECISION - MAKING

*"The successful man will profit from his mistakes
and try again in a different way."*
—Dale Carnegie

It is the need for action that produces decisions. When you are going through the process of making a decision as a church leader or administrator you should always ask yourself, "Is there a need to take an action?" If the answer is "yes," then there is the need to make a decision.

One Sabbath morning before I began my sermon, I decided to present an innovative proposal to the church. I was a little anxious about doing something that was not common. I knew that somehow it could change the course of the church and of my ministry. It was planned, but I was unsure of the results. That morning, I told the church members that I would like to present a proposal that would be very good for all of them, but it needed everyone's support in order to function properly.

They looked at me curiously seeming anxious to hear my proposal. I was unsure of the result, for it was a radical idea and at the same time a new experience for me.

We may not be certain about the future results of our decisions today, but when we try to do the right thing, for the right reason following biblical guidance, we have no reason to regret our decisions.

On the other hand, it is not enough to start doing things in a different way or adopting a new way of thinking, even when the new way of acting or thinking is better. Don't ever fall into the trap of thinking that because something is better it will automatically be successful. Remember that those who have innovative ideas will always be challenged by those who defend and protect the traditional way of doing things.

Wise leaders don't make decisions that are not theirs to make and don't waste time making decisions that do not have to be made.

RESISTANCE TO DECISIONS

Progress is a nice word, but change, its motivator, has its enemies. It isn't that we are afraid of change or that we are so in love with the old ways. It is that place in between that we fear. It's like being between trapezes, there's nothing to hold on to.

Any change, even a change for the better, is always accompanied by drawbacks and discomfort. Change is not made without inconvenience, even when it means improvement. Difficulties arise from people's fear of change. People often oppose a proposed model merely because they have not participated in planning it, or because it may have been planned by those whom they dislike. People resist

> **"Plans are only good intentions unless they immediately degenerate into hard work."**
>
> —*Peter Drucker*

change. More accurately, they resist being changed by other people. Resistance can take the form of either open hostility or covert sabotage of the decision-makers' efforts, and even the best designed strategy will fail if those who must carry it out refuse to do so.

HOW TO MAKE DECISIONS

Does anyone make the right decisions all the time? I wish! I would certainly have saved myself from taking some long hard roads over the years. Always remember that we are all fallible human beings; none of us is perfect, but when we learn from our mistakes it can lead to great personal growth! Remember that not making a decision is a decision *not to take action*.

Do you feel undecided and uncertain at the moment you have to make important decisions? Your success depends upon making wise decisions. Therefore, learn the best way to make decisions, for this is an essential skill. Our decisions define the course of our professional careers and the quality of our personal lives. Nevertheless, only a few people have the ability to make a decision carefully.

Making decisions can be intimidating and time-consuming. And while there's no easy way to just make them, the following tips can help you to make decisions.

• **Identify and analyze the problem**

What is it that you have to decide? Your first task is recognizing that a problem exists. Analyze your problem carefully. The way you conduct the process of decision making will make a great difference. To make the right decision you need to carefully analyze the problem, evaluating its complexity and trying as much as possible to avoid the potential for harm. Making a decision without really thinking can lead to a miserable result.

• **Seek other people's opinions**

After much reflection, try to obtain other people's perspectives in relation to the way they see the current situation. People who are on the outside usually have a better view of inside problems.

• **Evaluate the evidence/gather information.**

Learn more about the problem situation. Look for possible causes and solutions. Ask some questions such as: Where did the information come from? Does it represent various points of view? What biases could be expected from each source? How accurate is the information gathered? Is it fact or opinion?

• **Consider alternatives and implications.**

Draw conclusions from the gathered evidence and pose solutions. Then, weigh the advantages and disadvantages of each alternative. What are the costs, benefits, and consequences? What are the obstacles, and how can they be handled? Most important, what solution best serves your goals and those of your church? Here's where your creativity is especially important.

• **Eliminate options**

As you come to know the situation better, you will be able to easily cross out some options that you had considered as possible solutions. This is the fastest method to make decisions.

• **Follow your intuition**

Allow your experience and intuition to speak for itself. Remember that your entire life is controlled by decisions. Don't be afraid of making decisions.

• **Pay attention**

Pay attention and make sure your decision will not influence other decisions. It is very rare for a decision to remain isolated. Think about it in the context of the situation, for this will be of great help in keeping yourself on the right path.

• **Choose and implement the best alternative.**

Select an alternative and put it into action. Then, follow through on your decision by monitoring the results of implementing your plan.[1]

Decisions are an inevitable part of human activity. It requires the right attitude. Every problem, properly perceived, becomes an opportunity.

• **Ask God for wisdom**

An important quality of good leadership is the ability to think and plan what they want to do and where they want to go. The first step for a successful church plan is to seek the Lord. God's direction is paramount. Then, one needs to be willing to follow God's plan by exercising the wisdom He gives to all who submit themselves to His guidance.

> "If you don't know where you are going, you might wind up someplace else."
>
> —*Yogi Berra*

At such moments, seeking the Lord in prayer and allowing the Holy Spirit to illuminate your mind and guide your decision will certainly make a great difference. Never forget that "The fear of the Lord is the beginning of wisdom..." (Proverbs 9:10) and "If any of you lacks wisdom, he should ask of God..." (James 1:5).

Perhaps your church prefers to keep on doing what they have always done. However, we need to improve what we are already doing. This is what Peter F. Drucker teaches us when he says: "Do better what you already do reasonably well."

---

[1] Mary Ellen Guffey, *Business Communication: Process and Product*, (Cincinnati: South-Western College Publishing, 1996), Chapter 1.

4

THE DANGER OF NEGATIVITY

"The difference between a leader with vision and a leader without vision is that although both are in the same place, having the same visual perspective about something, one only sees what is obvious while the other sees a horizon that goes beyond what is physical."
—*Anonymous*

At my church, on the Sabbath I presented this new idea, I tried to communicate tranquility and trust. Then I explained to my congregation that from that day forward it would be "forbidden to gossip in church." Some members began to look at me surprised. Their expressions asked, "Where is the pastor going with this?" I then explained that, as the church pastor, I could not allow a member to speak ill about someone else in public, nor would I allow a member to come to me to speak ill about another member. In addition, I said that somehow we should eliminate our habit of criticism.

I recognized that our church community had many strong points and many indications of real spiritual growth. But there were some practical areas to which we had all paid insufficient attention. One of these was the human tendency to gossip, repeat rumors, to draw unsupported conclusions, and to get disaffected with others. I admit I was not innocent in this area. None of us were. It is important to admit that our ears love to hear gossip.

As I continued, I shared with my congregation two thoughts from Ellen G. White about the subject:

• "Those who do evil with their gossiping tongues, who sow discord by selfish ideas and thoughts, by any jealousies, evil surmising, or covetousness, they grieve the Holy Spirit of God, for they are working at cross purposes with God, instead of answering the purposes of Christ, instead of answering to the prayer of Christ that His disciples may be one as He is one with the Father. They are working entirely in the lines the enemy has marked out."[1]

• "A living church will not be a gossiping church, planting doubt, questioning, evil surmising, and jealousy in the hearts and minds of others. It will be an earnest, working church. The members will be the Lord's chosen vessels to carry the message of salvation to others. They will be His light bearers."[2]

Instructions such as these come from God, so that we spiritual leaders may share them with the church. How great the moral and spiritual harm our church has suffered as a result of gossip and criticism! How many people have been hurt and disappointed as a result of unkind words! Only eternity will reveal the results of such tragic evil.

> "The heart of a fool is in his mouth, but the mouth of the wise man is in his heart."
>
> —*Benjamin Franklin*

WHAT IS GOSSIP?

To gossip means to speak in a way which raises questions or doubts about others or their character. Gossiping is a conversation behind someone's back which puts him/her in a bad light. According to the Merriam-Webster Dictionary, slander means "malicious talk; to spread damaging information; to defame; to speak ill of." Slander is the work of the devil, and those who slander are on his team. In fact, the Bible says that Satan is called the "accuser of the brethren" (Revelation 12:10). Are you an accuser of the brethren too? Even though it may not be your intention, you are being used by the devil! According to Scripture, any Christian whose mouth is out of control does not have a right relationship with God. "If anyone considers himself religious and yet does not keep a tight reign on his tongue, he deceives himself, and his religion is worthless" (James 1:26).

"Gossip" also has a connotation of whispering. According to the same dictionary, "gossip" means "to indulge in idle talk or rumors about others; spreading of sensational stories." Funk and Wagnalls' dictionary defines it as "idle, or malicious talk about others." As we can see, gossiping is a close cousin to slander, and God's Word places both in the same [category] as murder and other wickedness—sins worthy of death.[3]

THE MOTIVATION FOR GOSSIPING

Compassion or sincere concern for someone is not an excuse for gossiping. No matter how pure or innocent the motive, raising questions about others still damages their reputation. Someone may say, "I am concerned about so and so." "I am having a problem with so and so." "I heard something about so and so. Do you know if that's true?" "Have you heard that so and so...?" "I know what I say is TRUE, so it is not gossiping." Where does the idea come from that words are gossip only if they are not true?[4]

The gossiper destroys another's reputation, whether intentionally or accidentally. The most famous excuse for gossiping is: "I only mentioned it because I was concerned." If personal concern excused gossiping, 90% of all gossiping could be justified. If those gossiping were genuinely concerned, they would have gone directly to the person they gossiped about, instead of raising doubts about him/her to someone else. God's solution for those who have concerns for another is for them to go to the one they say they are concerned about.

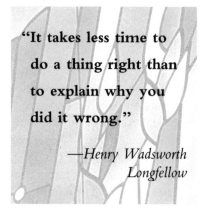

"It takes less time to do a thing right than to explain why you did it wrong."

—*Henry Wadsworth Longfellow*

Avoid associating with people who gossip: The Bible declares, "A gossiper betrays a confidence; so avoid a man who talks too much" (Proverbs 20:19). You probably remember the old saying: "If you can't say something good about others, don't say anything at all." Wise advice if you wish to avoid sin.

A gossiper thrives on the negative, the controversial, and the sensational. Any person who is genuinely concerned about solving a problem will go and privately confront the person at the source and express his concern. If it's more appropriate one should go privately to the pastor.

THE CHURCH CHALLENGE

Gossip in the church is becoming a real sin amongst us. If a community becomes full of gossip, allegation and counter-claims, very soon we will destroy ourselves. A house divided will fall. And don't think gossip is just words. Proverbs teaches that gossip stirs up dissension; but Proverbs

6:12-14 parallels "a corrupt mouth" with winking with the eye, signaling with the feet, motioning with the fingers (NIV). Our body language can effectively be gossip.

As gossip in the church spreads, it becomes distorted. The result is that when the victims hear it, they inevitably become angry, and often feel that they cannot associate with their brothers and sisters in the church if such things are thought about them. They are ashamed, angry because what was said was untrue, and tempted to become vindictive against those whom they hold to be responsible. In extreme cases, they leave church fellowship. As Solomon reminds us, "An offended brother is more unyielding than a fortified city" (Proverbs 18:19). Often, however the result is simply a decreased attendance at services, a breaking of close contact with the brothers and sisters who ought to be their true friends. This results in a church community which is cold and untrusting of each other, with everyone of us internalizing our struggles, appearing righteous on the surface but never opening our hearts.

Gossip and its effects sap the real spirituality of all involved. We have enough wonderful things to contemplate: the supremacy of the love of Christ, far above our human knowledge; the sublime intricacy of God's word and character; the fulfillment of prophecy; the wonder of our Hope. These things ought to fill our thinking and our conversation with each other. If they don't, and gossip in the church becomes the main diet of our conversation, something is seriously wrong with us. We have only a few years at most before we will stand before the judgment seat of Christ. We need to be using every moment.

Gossip and slander also disqualify persons for spiritual leadership (1 Timothy 3:11, James. 3:2). A gossiper often thrives upon secrecy. Where secrecy is removed, gossip is hampered. A gossiper always contributes to a problem and never to a solution. A gossiper always distorts and exaggerates, and is never a reliable source of truth. Those who gossip and slander are not in right fellowship with God (Romans 1:28-32). Those who gossip rarely get answers to prayer, and often face persistent, unexplainable problems (Psalms 66:18, Proverbs 21:23; 6:12-15).

WHAT TO DO ABOUT GOSSIPING

If you have been a gossiper, confess this sin and ask Christ to forgive you. "Repent" by turning in a new direction and surrendering your tongue to Christ, never to gossip or bad-mouth again (1 John 1:9, 1

Corinthians 7:10). Keep your nose out of other people's business. If you can't say something good or encouraging about others, then keep your mouth shut (Ephesians 4:29).

Avoid association with persons who gossip (Proverbs 20:19). Expose works of darkness by reporting gossipers to the pastor that he may confront and offer correction. Gossiping should be treated as any other vile sin (Ephesians 5:11). "I will watch my ways and keep my tongue from sin; I will put a muzzle on my mouth as long as the wicked are in my presence" (Psalms 39:1).[5]

PRACTICAL RESPONSE

If you feel you have been slandered by gossip in the church, remember that almost every servant of God has been through this at the hands of those they counted as their brethren: Joseph, Moses, Job, David, Jeremiah, Nehemiah, Paul, and, above all, the Lord Himself. Saul implied David and Jonathan were homosexual (1 Samuel 20:30); Miriam and Aaron implied Moses (their own brother!) was immoral (Numbers 12:1). The comment that Moses was the humblest man on earth is made in the very context of his enduring unjust criticism in a spiritual way (Numbers 12:3).

The way Paul commanded Timothy not to even consider a complaint against an elder unless another two or three had been eye-witnesses (1 Timothy 5:19) indicates that he expected elders to be slandered from within the ecclesia. The more you read between the lines of Paul's letters, the more evident it is that his very own brethren almost unbelievably (?) slandered him. Thus the Galatians whispered that Paul still preached circumcision (Galatians 5:11), probably basing that nasty rumor on the fact he had circumcised Timothy. He has to remind the Thessalonians that he isn't preaching because he wants to take money and have relationships with women (1 Thessalonians 2:3-12). There were some wealthy women in Thessalonica who accepted the Gospel (Acts 17:4), and no doubt gossip spread from this. We could almost conclude that being unfairly gossiped about is a characteristic of the true servant of God. Indeed, when Paul lists the things which confirm his apostleship, he lists not only his imprisonments and shipwrecks; he says that the fact he has been slandered is another proof that he is a servant of Christ (2 Corinthians 6:8)! None of these men quit the community because they had been slandered. They stuck it out, and so must we.

Being slandered drives us to the realization that our own protestations of innocence are never enough, and thereby we learn something about the whole process of justification, drawing closer to the Father and Son. If we run away, we are running away from the test which the Lord has given us in order to develop our faith in and love of Him. He will try to teach us the same humility another way; there can be no escape of the cross if we are to be His.

Avoiding what is negative in our church could seen like an impossible mission, but I challenge you to allow your mind to go beyond what today seems to be impossible to do. Remember there is nothing in our lives that God cannot accomplish. Make Him your partner and the architect of the dreams you have for your church; as you do this, you will become aware that yesterday's impossibility became today's reality.

---

[1] Ellen G. White, Letter 20, 1899.
[2] White, Manuscript Releases, vol. 21, p. 33.
[3] Dale A. Robbins, Article "What is wrong with gossip?"
[4] Melody Green, lastdays@lastdaysministries.org.
[5] *Ibid.*

5

APPLYING BIBLICAL PRINCIPLES

"The Bible is the great standard of right and wrong, clearly defining sin and holiness. Its living principles, running through our lives like threads of gold, are our only safeguard in trial and temptation."
—Ellen G. White

The Bible is the complete and absolute standard of right and wrong. It does not, however, directly describe every act we should avoid. It teaches principles we must apply. Biblical principles should be applied carefully when determining whether an act is right or wrong according to God's word.

When reinforcing the proposal I was presenting to my church members, I could not overlook what God tells us in the Bible. The principle in Matthew 18 comes to mind. Although you may be very familiar with this chapter, what is the application of this passage for our day? Is there any truth in Jesus' words that we can apply to our churches today? Matthew 18:15-20 says, "If your brother sins against you, go and show him his fault, just between the two of you. If he listens to you, you have won your brother over. But if he will not listen, take one or two others along, so that 'every matter may be established by the testimony of two or three witnesses.' If he refuses to listen to them, tell it to the church; and if he refuses to listen even to the church, treat him as you would a pagan or a tax collector. I tell you the truth, whatever you bind on earth will be bound in heaven, and whatever you loose on earth will be loosed in heaven. Again, I tell you that if two of you on earth agree about anything you ask for, it will be done for you by my Father in heaven. For where two or three come together in my name, there am I with them."

Here in this passage Jesus sets the standard by which we as Christians are to deal with those who sin against us individually. These verses relate specifically to sins committed between individual believers. Jesus is telling us how the conflicts between individual believers are to be resolved so that the believers may be reconciled with one another, alleviating strife and dissension. As Matthew 18:35 tells us, we are to forgive one another from the heart, and that forgiveness is not contingent upon whether or not the believer who has wronged us either apologizes or makes amends—we are to forgive unconditionally, as we have been forgiven by God.

> "Never look down on anybody, unless you are going to help them up."
>
> —Rev. Jesse Jackson

THE TWO OR THREE WITNESSES PRINCIPLE

The principle of "the testimony of two or three witnesses" is biblical. As a Christian church we need to base what we believe on the Bible. Consider the following passages to learn what the Bible teaches us:

• "A single witness shall not rise up against a man on account of any iniquity or any sin which he has committed; on the evidence of two or three witnesses a matter shall be confirmed" (Deuteronomy 19:15).

• "But if he does not listen to you, take one or two more with you, so that by the mouth of two or three witnesses every fact may be confirmed" (Matthew 18:16).

• "This is the third time I am coming to you. Every fact is to be confirmed by the testimony of two or three witnesses" (2 Corinthians 13:1).

• "Do not receive an accusation against an elder except on the basis of two or three witnesses" (1 Timothy 5:19).

In other words, the matters upon which the Church acts are matters that the Word of God has already judged, upon which the Law of God has already ruled. Principles of Scripture have been violated. They are not just opinion, but involve actions taken to deal with sin, where the verdict is rendered according to the Word of God.

Notice that in Matthew 18 it calls for two or three people to go with you to witness what transpires when you meet the person in question. This also suggests that when there is factionalism, with people taking sides, two or three witnesses from each side should attend the meeting.

The point of this is the establishment of truth by two or three witnesses. These witnesses can confirm the truth of the conversation that will ensue, but their primary purpose is to help convince the offender to repent.

THREE IMPORTANT STEPS

Although there are many scriptures that deal with this issue, the two main ones, which show how to deal with brothers who are at fault, are found in Matthew 18 and Galatians 6.

The First Step: There is never to be a standing investigatory committee or an oversight group responsible for ferreting out sin. As we grow spiritually and as we grow in intimacy and fellowship with the believers, we will naturally become aware of what is going on in others' lives. As we grow in Christ and we discover anyone in a trespass or if we see a brother sinning, we are then called to act on his behalf. It is important to note that all of us, not just the elders and leaders, are called to this ministry. If you are the one who sees a brother in trespass, you are responsible for going to the brother and speaking with him. Don't go to the pastors or local elders; go to the offending brother. The only qualification given for the person confronting is that he be a brother and that he be spiritual, indwelt by the Spirit of the Living God.

If the Lord has chosen you to be used in this approach, the first step is to pray and check the motivation. Are we motivated by love for the brother? Are we operating in a spirit of gentleness? Are we trying to restore him? Are we being careful, in case we are tempted in a like manner? Obviously, there is much to be prayed about and considered before we take the first step of talking privately with the sinning brother.

Having prepared yourself through prayer and self examination, the next step is to go privately to the sinning brother, "showing him his fault in private." I am convinced that this is the Lord's choice method. It springs from the fact that most discipline is personal and private and provides a bridge between personal and public discipline. Jesus was specific in using the words "in private." How wonderful that the Lord even cares if we get embarrassed, and deliberately and specifically tried to protect us from the further embarrassment of public notice. What opportunity for quick and private repentance. When successful, this first step of public discipline brings the sinner to repentance, edifies the body, and usually strengthens the relationship between the one confronting and the brother being confronted.

Time must be allowed for the Holy Spirit to convict and convince. Most people's initial reaction is not their final reaction. Give the person some room to prayerfully consider what you have brought to his or her attention. Do not put a timetable on the work of the Holy Spirit but continue to make yourself available for prayer and counsel. Don't expect an initial response to be immediate repentance. It is a privilege to observe the Holy Spirit working in a person's life. A good rule of thumb is to give the person as much time as you would want someone to give you.

If the person listens to you, you have won him or her. The matter is finished and no further confrontation is necessary. Careful consideration must be given to the fruits of repentance to make sure that the person is sincere and is taking biblical steps to move away from the occasion of temptation. Continued prayer and counsel may be necessary. Both should be offered until both the confronting person and the offending person are convinced that victory has been achieved.

The Second Step: What do we do if the person refuses to listen and refuses to repent? Jesus said, "if he will not listen, take one or two others along, so that 'every matter may be established by the testimony of two or three witnesses.'" There has been much written on the second step in public church discipline. Some suggest that the two or more witnesses be witness to the original trespass. Others believe that the two or more witness are there to witness the people as they confront the sin issue, determining the attitude and responses of the two involved in confrontation. This step definitely takes the process out of the private arena into the public. It is a dramatic escalation of the process and is designed to bring public pressure on the person to quit sinning and repent.

With two or three witnesses, we are to go to the sinning individual. Who should these witnesses be? I don't believe they have to be witnesses to the act of sin, but they are to be witnesses to the confrontation. The witnesses should also be spiritual and well grounded in the Word, ones who will not be tempted in the area of sin. They should also have a relationship with both parties. They are there to observe the process and to offer counsel to both the confronter and the person being confronted. Because these confrontations sometimes get emotional and fiery, the witnesses can also act as mediators to make sure that there is a spirit of gentleness. While the person who is confronting the one in offense is speaking, the two or three witnesses are to help keep the goal of restoration in mind and to keep the conversation going in the right direction.

The person being confronted may sometimes try to change the focus by obfuscating, attacking the person or persons who are confronting him or her, offering excuses for the continued behavior or outright denial of the charges. The witnesses are to help both parties remain calm, to keep the conversation focused on restoration, to make sure that the motivation of love for the person is clearly communicated as the motive for the confrontation and to move the conversation towards a decision.

The Third Step: If, after being confronted privately and then with two or three witnesses, there is no fruit of repentance, the original confronter and the witnesses are to report it to the church committee. This is not the local church or the local group who meets in fellowship but only the church committee. The reporting should include the nature of the sin, the steps that have already been taken, and the results of the previous conversations.

The goal of restoration must be adhered to even more arduously in the very public disclosures since the possibility for wrong thinking and action increases with the number of brothers and sisters involved, and wrong attitudes. The goal is restoration, not crucifixion of the erring person. All members of the local body are now involved in confronting and helping the brother.[1]

MORE INSPIRED INSTRUCTIONS

Ellen White also talks about this subject. It is worthwhile to read some of her counsels, for there is no doubt the church is in danger when we don't follow God's clear instructions regarding this subject.

• "The Bible plan of avoiding and remedying difficulties among brethren is the only safe plan. Christ is grieved to see some disregarding this instruction, following their own plans—plans opposed to His. When those who claim to be Christians work in harmony with divine instruction, there will be far less evil-surmising and evil-speaking in the church."[2]

• "If you think that a brother is doing what's wrong, go right to him. Do not go to someone else, because this will not cure the difficulty. Go to the very one whom you think is in error, and ask him if he is standing in a position that will lead others to make missteps. Tell him that he must make straight paths for his feet, lest the lame be turned out of the way."[3]

• "The work done at haphazard in the church by speaking to others of errors and mistakes before speaking to the one at fault has been the greatest cause and manifestation of wickedness and apostasy in the church. Weakness has come to many because they have not taken up their appointed work. God will not accept your gifts, however precious they may be, unless you make a straight path for your feet by following the directions that Christ has given."[4]

The Bible also suggests that problems among the brethren should be resolved before one worships God. "Therefore, if you are offering your gift at the altar and there remember that your brother has something against you, leave your gift there in front of the altar. First go and be reconciled to your brother; then come and offer your gift" (Matthew 5:23-24).

We have enough inspired counsel to do what's right. If mistakes were committed in the past due to not following God's instructions, it is time to learn from them. When we learn from them, we will change our actions and behavior.

That Sabbath morning in my church, as I presented the proposal, I assumed my own posture of commitment with God before the church members. I knew that a change had to start with me and then with the way I was leading the church. Jacob Braude states, "Consider how hard it is to change yourself and you'll understand what little chance you have in trying 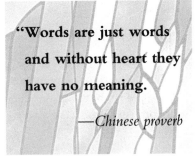 to change others." To expect the church to change without having its leadership assume a new posture is a miracle we haven't seen lately.

"**Words are just words and without heart they have no meaning.**

—*Chinese proverb*

As part of my personal commitment and example, I announced that even at Church Committee meetings it would be forbidden to gossip, because I was aware that occasionally church committees are preferred places to speak badly of others.

RULES AND PRINCIPLES

A principle motivates you internally to do the things that seem good and right. People also develop principles by living with people who live by principle, seeing the real benefits of such a life.

A rule externally compels you, through force, threat or punishment, to do the things someone else has deemed good or right. People follow or break rules.

Which is the hope most parents have for their kids? Do they hope their kids will comply with and follow rules, or do they hope their kids will live their lives making choices that are good and right?

Most people have heard somewhere, at sometime, "we have to have rules" and they swallowed it because they were punished if they didn't. And so here they are today, talking about rules without any thought to what rules really are.

It seems to me that rules control others and principles guide them. Hence, if I have rules, I don't have to think for myself. Like in a school setting—bells rings, stand up, move, sit down, write this, look here, and look there—all very rule bound.

Principles, on the other hand, are guides to respectful living, freedom, and openness. We can value completely different interpretations of the principles.

THE JOY OF "DOING THINGS RIGHT"

I gazed in the eyes of the church members and could see that they loved the idea. Their expressions showed approval as well as a decision that they would support the new idea. The church youth really embraced the new concept. When they were playing soccer on Sundays and someone committed a hard fault and the person who was hit got ready to mutter or complain, someone would advise, "Don't say anything; don't say anything, because here in the ball field it is also forbidden to gossip or make public criticism. If you have something to say against your brother, go in private and tell him. We don't need to hear what you have to say."

> "People may doubt what you say, but they will believe what you do."
>
> —*Lewis Cass*

Some people make little progress in their lives or work generally because they have little or no concept of DOING THINGS RIGHT. Sometimes people who are generally intelligent and competent make little or no progress in a particular area because they haven't learned to do things right in that area.

"Doing things right" can be a touchy topic. I'm fallible like everyone else. From time to time I make my share of dumb mistakes. Fortunately, I try to learn from my mistakes and do better next time.

One thing I know. Good leaders make a difference in their community, not so much by what they say as by what they do. A leader will always be an example to be followed. Therefore, an expression of love from a leader may be something beautiful and moving, but an expression of love is not necessarily love in action. The fulfillment of these intentions, dreams, and longings requires doing things right, being led by principles and maybe involving a personal commitment and sacrifice.

---

[1] Mike Indest. Article: "The motivation of discipline."

[2] Ellen G. White, "Bible Training School," *Preach the Truth,* July 1, 1903, paragraph 3.

[3] Ellen G. White, "Notes of Travel—The College View Council," *Review and Herald,* January 19, 1905, paragraph 7.

[4] *Ibid.* paragraph 9.

6

THE CHALLENGE OF CHANGE

"How much life and energy are you investing in your dreams?"
—*Carl Roberts*

I believe that you can make big changes in your life in as little as a year. In order to do that, you must decide what is most important to you and be willing to stop doing all the other things that waste your time and energy and divert you from your primary destination.

You don't have to be single-minded about it; everyone should have a well-rounded life. But if you want your dreams to come true, you must identify them, plan how to reach them, and never lose sight of your destination.

Act on your dream! You can be a very different person—the person you want to be—a year from now.

As a church leader do you have some dreams for your church? Are you trying to fulfill them? Certainly, your dreams may become reality if they are in tune with God's dream for you.

DO NOT BE AFRAID OF CHALLENGES

Change can be a difficult thing for many of us, whether it's personal change or professional change. However we all know that change happens. It's thrust upon us, it happens to us, and we make it happen. Given its inevitability, it's probably best to accept change and rise to the challenge, even embrace it. And that's a lot easier to do when you're prepared with the knowledge and tools for managing it.

One of my dreams was to grow in a loving church, free from criticism and negativity. As I began to implement my plan to eliminate criticism and gossip, the first great challenge was to plan the next church committee meeting. How could I conduct a meeting without including negative talk about anyone? Critical comments had become common in such meetings. I prayed about it, reflected, and planned. The church committee met once a month to discuss church matters. We were planning to choose a new elder at the next meeting. I had butterflies in my stomach just thinking about the challenge before me. After all, changing an old habit, like changing the course of a river, wouldn't be easy.

When we venture into the unknown, perhaps the most consistent and successful strategy is to be open to new situations that may arise. When we are willing to adapt, change becomes our friend.

A great temptation in leadership is to run away from commitments, especially when the leader sees the challenges ahead. It is always easy to present convincing excuses to avoid taking responsibility. The day will come, however, when the excuses seem so trivial and inconsequential that we'll regret losing precious opportunities. No matter how difficult the effort may be, such difficulty is only temporary. Nevertheless, it is worth the effort.

> "It is not how much you do, but how much love you put into the doing that matters."
>
> —*Mother Teresa*

A FISH STORY

I read a story on the internet which can illustrate the good result of challenges. You have probably heard that the Japanese have always loved fresh fish. But the waters close to Japan have not held many fish for decades. So to feed the Japanese population, fishing boats got bigger and went further than ever. The further the fishermen went, the longer it took to bring in the fish. If the return trip took more than a few days, the fish were not fresh. The Japanese did not like the taste.

To solve this problem, fishing companies installed freezers on their boats. They would catch the fish and freeze them at sea. Freezers allowed the boats to go farther and stay longer. However, the Japanese could taste the difference between fresh and frozen, and they did not like frozen fish. The frozen fish brought a lower price. So fishing companies installed fish tanks. They would catch the fish and place them in the tanks. After a little thrashing around, the fish stopped moving. They were tired and dull, but alive.

Unfortunately, the Japanese could still taste the difference. Because the fish did not move for days, they lost their fresh-fish taste. The Japanese preferred the taste of fresh fish, not sluggish fish. So how did Japanese fishing companies solve this problem? How do they get fresh-tasting fish to Japan?

They add a small shark to each tank. The shark eats a few fish, but most of the fish arrive in a very lively state. The fish are challenged. So, put a shark in your tank and see how far you can really go!

Don't get inactive; don't get intimidated. Accept the challenge and courageously embrace the opportunity. Maybe that's what you need to face today. Do not be afraid. The biblical promise affirms: "Commit your way to the Lord; trust in him and he will do this" (Psalm 37:5).

THE CHALLENGE OF THE FIRST COMMITTEE

Finally the church committee meeting day arrived. A good number of members were present, and I believe most of them didn't remember the commitment we had made in church. Perhaps this is one of the reasons we make mistakes in leadership. We easily forget the commitments we make with the church, or we do not persevere in following plans that have been decided.

I reminded the committee members that we were meeting to make some decisions and that as church representatives we should do our best as we studied and analyzed each item in the agenda. I reminded them of our commitment that during church committee meetings we would be examples in maintaining the good reputation of all members. Therefore, we should keep our promise and not make negative comments.

The committee members agreed to the little instruction I gave, although they had no idea how things were going to take place. After all, we were about to begin to change a strongly rooted habit in the church. It would be an historical event for our congregation.

I suppose in everybody's minds there was the question: How do we participate in a church committee without saying anything negative?

PRACTICE WHAT YOU BELIEVE

The crucial moment at the committee meeting had arrived. Choosing a new elder was a challenge. At these moments, as leaders, we have to be sure of how to proceed. The more our goals are real and clear, the more efficient we will be in the way we reach them.

That day I asked the committee members to suggest names for that important church office. Some names were mentioned and written on the board. The names I'll use here are fictitious, but the example describes the reality I lived on that historic day in my ministry.

1. Peter
2. John
3. Joseph

As we began to consider the names, I asked if someone had any positive comments to make about the first name, Peter. Everyone was quiet. They were not used to working that way. In the past, in a similar situation, some would surely make negative comments about the names being proposed. But now the situation was different. Because they were not used to that change in the procedure, there was absolute silence. Everyone was being challenged to think and act in a different way.

> "Have a heart that never hardens, a temper that never tires, a touch that never hurts."
>
> —*Charles Dickens*

Challenges inspire innovation. They force us to look at things from different perspectives; they motivate us to come out of lethargy; they help us to persevere when we face hardship. Challenge yourself, because a great challenge will force you to be a better leader.

BREAKING THE SILENCE AND THE TRADITION

Silence was broken when someone lifted his hand and said, "Pastor, I have something to say about Brother Peter," and with a certain fear of making a mistake in his comment, he cautiously said, "He is a church member." I quickly commended that comment by saying that it was an important and positive detail. I thanked him for his contribution. You may be thinking that I wasn't sincere, but I was. In fact, many times, church committees appoint people who are not regular church members for a church office although the *Seventh-day Adventist Church Manual* forbids it.

Church leaders should know well the *Church Manual*. It is an important source of information for those who want to lead effectively and safely. Church leaders should be committed to the orientation presented there because it is the result of years of study and decision by a representative church. It is a source of information that has been accumulated throughout the years. Besides, it reflects the supreme decision of a world church. We cannot neglect its orientations. As leaders we are church representatives, not merely defenders of our own concepts and ideas. Knowing the *Church Manual* well will help us to better maintain unity and coherence in administrative and ministerial procedures.

After that first contribution, another hand was raised and the person said, "Pastor, Brother Peter is married." "Very good," I responded, although I knew that to be a church elder there is no need to be married. The Bible and the *Church Manual* do not set forth such a requirement.

After those two positive observations, there was silence again in the meeting room. I asked if anyone else had a positive comment to make about the first name. No one wanted to say anything else. I had understood the message through that silence, and I believe they understood as well. Sometimes there is power in silence. Therefore, keeping silence in the church committee about certain subjects is to act wisely. There is also prudence and truth in silence.

Because there were no more comments about the first name (Peter), I suggested we consider the second name. Now we had Brother John's name. I asked them to make observations. One person raised his hand and said: "Besides being married and having two teenage children, our brother John relates well to the church youth." I was happy with that comment, for we were creating a new way of approaching and commenting about the names being analyzed. We were facing the challenge before us with a Christian attitude. Someone else added, "We work in the same company, and everyone there calls him 'pastor' because he is always trying to preach the gospel to others." It was another very good quality. I asked again, "Anything else?" After some other positive comments, someone concluded by saying, "Our brother John has always attended church meetings, he is very committed to the church activities he's involved in, and he has the ability to speak in public." After hearing all contributions and comments about John, we moved on to the last name, Joseph.

7

MAINTAIN CHRISTIAN ETHICS

"Before cursing your problems, keep in mind that they are what bring value and meaning to your accomplishments."
—*Walter Rodman*

Often God uses problems to prepare us for something much better. Every problem has a peculiar way of molding virtues such as patience, trust, perseverance, self-control and kindness (James 1:2-3). Problems also discipline the mind. The best kind of problem is that which strengthens our character, and shows us who we really are and what we can do. Better still, problems build and consolidate our faith.

Let's go back to the last name being considered by the church committee. Brother Joseph was a very popular church member. He was known by everyone for being extroverted and for his ability to make friends. However, he had some problems: he did not pay tithe, he drank alcoholic beverages, and when he lost his temper, he was violent with his wife.

On the other hand, what if that brother Joseph had been a committee member? In such cases, I always try to instruct the group in advance that when someone has a negative observation about someone present who is nominated, that person should leave the room with the person whose name is being considered. This enables them to talk privately, following the biblical principle of Matthew 18. It also gives the members more freedom to make comments, even though we were committed to saying only positive things about the person.

Now consider the fact that only the church pastor knows brother Joseph's problems. In such cases, when he is not in the committee I excuse myself, go out and talk to him privately. I inform him that he has been nominated to be a church elder, but because he does not pay tithes, drinks alcoholic beverages, and is violent towards his wife, he would not be the best qualified person to be a spiritual leader of the church at the moment. I remind him that because I choose not to make negative comments to the committee, I'm trying to follow the biblical counsel, discussing this with him in private. I also tell him I want to preserve his image before the church, and that he needs spiritual assistance. I promise to help him, but at the moment, as local pastor, I have to solve the problem in an "ecclesiastical" manner. So I advise him to withdraw his name from nomination for church elder.

After this pastoral conversation, I go back to the committee meeting, not mentioning a thing about what we talked about outside. When all the names are considered and comments ended, I suggest that everyone use a piece of paper to indicate one name among the three names proposed. I instruct them once more that they should think and choose the best name. Brother Joseph raises his hand and requests permission to speak. He makes the following request, "I would like to ask that my name be removed for consideration for personal reasons." As pastor, I may even act surprised, asking him if he is sure of his decision. He certainly is. I accept his request in the form of a proposal, and ask if everyone agrees. Once it is agreed, his name is taken off the list.

> "When I do good, I feel good; when I do bad, I feel bad. That's my religion."
>
> —*Abraham Lincoln*

A SIMPLE TRUTH

We proceed to the voting process with only two names. In your opinion, whom do you think will be selected by the committee to be the new elder? I believe your answer was John. Am I correct? But why him? Certainly because he is better qualified than the other candidate. This way, a simple and great truth becomes evident: Yes, it is possible to appoint someone to a church office without negative comments. If it is possible to nominate someone for his/her qualities, why then do we mention people's weaknesses on these occasions? Doesn't it seem conflicting and incoherent? We need to awaken to this truth! People are not elected because they have fewer problems, but because they possess qualities to fill the position. How different church committees would be if this simple and basic concept were put into action!

Let's just imagine the possibility of brother Joseph not being present at the committee meeting and his name receiving many commendations. After all, he is a popular person and his problems are not known. It seems he is going to be appointed to be a future church elder. But there is someone at the committee who knows about Joseph's problems. He knows, however, that he should not make any negative comments. Nevertheless, seeing that Joseph is being nominated, he raises his hand and says, "Pastor, I've been silent the whole time, but I believe I should provide some information about Joseph for the good of the church." I quickly ask if it is something positive. "Unfortunately not," our well intentioned brother answers. With much love, but also with assurance, I say that in this case he should remain silent.

Suppose that Joseph is nominated by the church committee to be a church elder despite all his personal and spiritual problems. Is there a problem? Maybe it is a big problem for your church, but not for mine. Let me explain. The church committee does not have the final word for an appointment. The final word always depends upon a vote from the church gathered in assembly. Usually, when we present the nominations, there is a first reading, and after a week, a second reading. We do this to give the church members time to think about the names and make observations. In other words, the presentation of a name by the church committee is not the final word in someone's nomination for a church office.

However, the person who wanted to present relevant information publicly at the church committee, and was denied, now has the opportunity to go to Joseph's home for a private conversation.

Imagine this brother following the principle set forth in Matthew 18. The concern needs to be raised. So, his responsibility is to talk with the brother in private. He visits Joseph and honestly says that the reason for his visit is the fact that Joseph's name was presented by the committee for the office of church elder, but there is behavior which should prevent him from holding such office. The fact that he does not pay God's tithe, he drinks alcoholic beverages, and is violent with his wife disqualifies him for such an office. This brother might offer Joseph spiritual assistance, but at the moment, he first needs to see that the problem is solved in an "ecclesiastical" manner. He may even suggest that

Joseph ask to have his name removed from the second reading.

In situations like this, an honest person will not object to such counsel. He/she will appreciate the visit, the ethical conduct of the church officer, and may even ask him to be the spokesperson to the pastor regarding his request. I can assure you that in 25 years of ministry, I've never found a member who answered: "I'm going to continue with wrong doing, and I also want to be a spiritual leader of the church."

> "It is more important to be kind than to be right."
>
> —Jan Paulsen

SUPPORTING, NOT FIXING

Wesley Snipes says, "The person who seeks to change another person in a relationship basically sets the stage for a great deal of conflict." This is often true. When people contact others with the intention of simply pointing out their errors, criticizing or changing them, they end up forgetting or ignoring that their role in a Christian or social relationship is not to change one another, but to offer mutual support (Ezekiel 3:17-19).

The concept of "fixing" usually implies telling the other person what's wrong with him or her. In fact, that is the time to support one another, which means to remain on his/her side when things go wrong.

Attempting fix someone may cause negative reactions and produce hostility. "Support" means to healthfully nourish the relationship, knowing that things have the potential to get better. As you develop this mutual support system in Christian life, you will be promoting a healthy relationship.

THE TEST OF THE THREE STRAINERS

A friend of mine sent me, an interesting story by email about a new priest who arrived at Saint Augustine Parish. This story can teach how we need to be careful about how we share information about others.

On the first day, Mrs. Flora went to see him. "Father, you can't believe what I was told about John…" She didn't even get to the end of her sentence because the priest interrupted her.

"Wait a minute, Mrs. Flora, has what you're about to tell me been tested through the three strainers?"

"Strainers? What strainers, father?"

"The first strainer is truth. Are you sure this is absolutely true?"

"No, how could I be? All I know is they told me, but I think that…"

"Well, then your story went through the first strainer. Let's go to the second strainer, kindness. Is what you're about to tell me something you would like others to say about you?"

"Of course not! Never!"

"Then your story went through the second strainer, too. Let's go to the third strainer, which is need. Do you really think you need to tell me this fact or even tell other people?"

"No, father, there is no need."

Mrs. Flora left the church ashamed.

Before you talk about someone, test it through the three strainers: if the fact goes through one of them, it is best to be quiet. Is what you are going to say true? Are you going to say it with kindness? Do you think it needs to be said? These questions can also help you to consider comments made to you in church.

CONSISTENCY AND ETHICS

Consistency—the absence of contradictions—has sometimes been called the hallmark of ethics. Ethics is supposed to provide us with a guide for moral living, and to do so it must be rational, and to be rational it must be free of contradictions.

Ethics requires consistency in the sense that our moral standards, actions, and values should not be contradictory. Examining our lives to uncover inconsistencies and then modifying our moral standards and behaviors so that they are consistent is an important part of moral development.

A more important kind of inconsistency is that which can emerge when we apply our moral standards to different situations. To be consistent, we must apply the same moral standards to one situation that we apply to another unless we can show that the two situations differ in relevant ways.

So central is consistency to Christian ethics that some moralists have held that it is the whole of ethics. They have argued that if people consistently treat all human beings the same, they will always act ethically. Ethical behavior, they argue, is simply a matter of being consistent by extending to all persons the same respect and consideration that we claim for ourselves. The Bible itself seems to imply that ethics consist of nothing more than consistency with the words: "Do unto others as you would have them do unto you: this is the whole Law and the prophets" (Matthew 7:12). This Bible verse sometimes has been interpreted as meaning that all of morality can be summed up in the requirement to avoid contradictions between what one thinks is appropriate for others and what one thinks is appropriate for oneself.

Ethics also requires a consistency between our ethical standards and our actions, as well as among our inner desires. Finally, ethics requires that there be consistency between how we treat ourselves and how we treat others.

POSITIVE WORDS ARE HEALING

Did you know we spend less energy to say a positive word than a negative one? Research indicates that when we say positive words, even in difficult or problematic situations, our body relaxes. As we relax, the blood flow to our brain increases. A well oxygenated brain has more probability of thinking with creativity, making wise decisions, finding rational solutions, and producing answers to questions, even the most difficult ones.

Positive words facilitate relationships and create a peaceful atmosphere, which provides rest, easiness, rejuvenation, and sleep, all needed for good health. Isn't it interesting?

On the other hand, contrary to popular concepts, negative words do not reduce tension. To open one's heart may be good in a few circumstances, but most of the time it's nothing more than lack of emotional control. To give vent to one's anger, not respecting the limits of good sense and good companionship, will only bring embarrassment and harm, both emotional and social.

A continuous stream of negative words creates problems in personal relationships, producing an atmosphere of disharmony, agitated sleep, and tattered nerves, all harmful to our health. One of the things we can do for our health is to change the way we speak!

I could not forget to mention the beautiful prayer of Saint Francis of Assisi, which serves us well as a daily devotional:

"O Lord,
Make me an instrument of Thy Peace!
Where there is hatred, let me sow love;
Where there is injury, pardon;
Where there is discord, harmony;
Where there is doubt, faith;
Where there is despair, hope;
Where there is darkness, light, and
Where there is sorrow, joy.

O, Divine Master, grant that I may not
so much seek to be consoled as to console;
to be understood as to understand;
to be loved as to love;
for it is in giving that we receive;
it is in pardoning that we are pardoned;
and it is in dying that we are born to Eternal Life."

The following questions are for your personal contemplation. It may help you to understand the importance of our words in church leadership.

DO YOU CONTROL YOUR WORDS?

1. Do you believe in the power of words?
   a) Yes   b) No

2. When you're emotional, do you usually say things without thinking?
   a) Yes   b) No

3. Are your words usually positive ones?
   a) Yes   b) No

4. Do you often talk about others without knowing if what you're saying is true?
   a) Yes   b) No

5. Do people consider you someone who is very talkative?
   a) Yes   b) No

6. When you hear a juicy story about someone, can you hardly wait to tell it to someone else?
    a) Yes   b) No

7. Do you easily keep secrets?
    a) Yes   b) No

8. No matter how carefully you try to control yourself, do you always sense you have talked more than you should?
    a) Yes   b) No

9. When you give a message to someone, do you always verify if they understood it?
    a) Yes   b) No

10. Are you consistently careful to maintain the image and good name of people?
    a) Yes   b) No

8

ETHICS IN CONTROL

"In every situation you may take countless positive actions, which are capable of helping you face those over which **you have no control."**
—Tim Kirk

When in church committees people face circumstances that are beyond their control, they may remain undecided and appear distressed. This sometimes generates frustration. However some members understand that if they use what they are able to control, circumstances will favor them.

For example, long ago people understood that it is impossible to control the seasons. However, some people understood that if they exerted control and did the appropriate things in various seasons, they could plant seeds that would grow and produce crops.

Do not concentrate on what is beyond your control. On the contrary, exercise control over your thoughts and your actions.

In a traditional church committee, when the leader loses control of the situation, or lacks knowledge and ethical ability to conduct the meeting, unexpected awkward situations may occur. When people are allowed to say anything they want about others, the results may be disastrous. People hurt others or are themselves hurt. As a matter of conscience, at the end of the meeting some pastors or elders ask the members to maintain secrecy about everything that was discussed. But can you imagine any committee where everyone really maintains secrecy? So why do we kid ourselves by asking for secrecy in church committees?

When I began our plan to avoid negative comments, many problems I had faced before disappeared completely. I didn't need to ask for secrecy regarding negative comments about nominees for church office. There was no need to threaten those who would open their mouths and tell details about what was discussed in the meetings because everything we had discussed or talked about was good. If members wanted to tell the details we discussed to someone else, they would be doing us a favor.

LEAVE CONTRADICTIONS BEHIND

Church committees usually begin with a prayer in which God's presence and the Holy Spirit's direction are requested. The problem starts when negative comments are made, many times with the best of intentions. How much unnecessary cruelty is inflicted at these times! I believe that at such moments God's presence is no longer felt. I imagine the enemy is delighted to be present at some church committees and might say to himself, "This is how I like it: they began the meeting in the name of God, but are going to end it in my name."

Let's imagine that the church committee I described had ended and that brother Joseph had not participated because he was not a member. He knows that every time someone is nominated for an office, his name is discussed and many people make negative comments. This makes him very upset with the church leadership. When he meets someone coming from the committee, he asks: "Did you choose anyone for church office today?"

"Yes!" the member answers.

"And what did the committee say about me?"

"Nothing!"

"Nothing?" pleads Joseph. "Does that mean the pastor asked for secrecy?"

"No."

"Then tell me what they said about me."

"OK, I'm going to tell you. They said you are a church member and that you are married."

"Is that it?"

"Yes."

Members who in the past were upset about comments made at the church committee now are impressed because no one talks negatively about them any more. Can you see the advantages of this Christian way of leading a church committee?

REAPING GOOD RESULTS

Now imagine a different scene. Suppose brother John was not at the committee meeting either. He is outside the committee room and when he sees the first person leaving the meeting room, he asks: "Anything new at the committee today?"

"Yes, we nominated a new elder."

"And who was nominated?"

"You, John. And I must say, I didn't know you, but after hearing so many positive comments about you, I'm proud to know you will be a leader at our church."

Can you see, once more, the difference? An atmosphere of respect, kindness and appreciation begins to be felt in the church.

Ghandi once said, "No act of kindness, no matter how small, is ever wasted." It is easy to act with kindness and understanding toward those who have been gentle and kind to us. However, the power of kindness is most clearly expressed when it is shown towards someone who does not deserve it.

Of course, there will always be those who will not react positively to such gestures. Nevertheless, do act with kindness, understanding and respect. Even though others may not respond to your attitude, you will benefit. And if someone is sensible enough to accept and appreciate your kindness, that's even better. "Do not be overcome by evil, but overcome evil with good" (Romans 12:21).

> "Ethics thought out is religious thought; ethics felt out is religious feeling, and ethics lived out is the religious life."
>
> —*William C. Gannett*

CUT EVIL AT ITS ROOT

I remember attending a committee meeting to appoint church officers for the following ecclesiastical year. When a name was proposed, the church treasurer raised his hand and said, "This person cannot be appointed because he does not pay God's tithes." I confess that such a thoughtless comment made me very sad. After that meeting I asked the treasurer, "Who gives you the right to publicly announce who returns tithe and who doesn't?" He seemed to forget that the information was confidential. No one is authorized to comment about it publicly. If a member is not returning the tithe for some reason, it is the treasurer's or Stewardship director's job to go to the home for a spiritual visit and approach the matter.

Our greatest motivation for not putting others in bad light is our obedience to the Law of Christ. We must love others as we want to be loved. If we do not want people to talk evil about us when we are not there, then we must treat them with the same consideration.

As children of God, we must be alert to one of Satan's chief goals to bring division to God's family. Offenses will happen in all relationships, so we must guard ourselves against harboring resentment, and sitting in judgment of one another. We must be especially careful not to fall victim to the devil's scheme and speak negatively of one another. Christ's prescription in Matthew 18 must be followed. Before mentioning our concern to anyone else, we must speak first to the one whose behavior concerns us. We must "be kind and compassionate to one another, forgiving each other, just as in Christ God forgave us" (Ephesians 4:32).

AVOIDING MISJUDGING

After the meeting in which the treasure had revealed too much about a member, I sought the treasurer in private and gave him guidance on how to handle such a matter. Church treasurers need to practice the principle set forth in Matthew 18. A few days after that meeting, I went to visit the brother whom the treasurer had mentioned was not returning tithe. Among the many subjects we talked about, I asked him if he was facing any financial problem, for I had noticed he was not returning God's tithes. He lowered his head. Looking at me with sadness and shame, he said, "Pastor, I should have talked to you earlier, but I did not have the chance before. I haven't had a job for six months now. As soon as I find a job, I will continue returning the tithe." I felt so awful at that moment, for many times people or church committee members speak in haste and end up blemishing a member's name just because they do not follow Mathew 18.

It is good to remember that when a church member is out of a job, and has no income, the church still considers him or her a faithful member. But how can one be a faithful giver if they have no income? The answer is simple: when one receives nothing, one returns 10% of nothing. This may seem to be word play, but it is true.

It has been common in some church nominating committees to have the treasurer act as a "financial inspector," saying who is and who isn't paying tithe. And they do it with a certain pride, as someone who's in control. This practice needs to be eliminated from the church, for we are not only committing unfairness, but also ignoring a biblical principle. In order to prevent this, the one chairing the committee should thoroughly understand the correct procedures.

HOW WE TREAT ONE ANOTHER

In "*The Leadership Compass*," a quarterly e-newsletter designed to help teachers and principals discuss the teaching and learning going on in their schools, John Wilcox and Susan Ebbs write, "Moral behavior is concerned primarily with the interpersonal dimension of our behavior: how we treat one another individually and in groups—and, increasingly, other species and the environment." The key here is that morality brings us into contact with others and asks us to consider the quality of that contact.

How many times have we asked ourselves: Is that the way I should treat someone else? Is that the way someone else should treat me? Ethics poses questions about how we ought to act in relationships and how we should live with one another. Ethics asks us to consider whether our actions are right or wrong. It also asks us how those character traits that help humans flourish (such as integrity, honesty, faithfulness, and compassion) play out in everyday living.

Thomas Shanks, S.J., in his article "Everyday Ethics," published on the Internet, says that people need a systematic way to approach living an ethical life. He shares five questions that, used daily, can help with the how-to of everyday morality.

1. Did I practice any virtues today? In *The Book of Virtues*, William Bennett notes that virtues are "habits of the heart" we learn through models—the loving parent or aunt, the demanding teacher, the respectful manager, the honest shopkeeper. They are the best parts of ourselves.

Ask yourself, did I cross a line today that gave up one of those parts? Or was I, at least some of the time, a person who showed integrity, trustworthiness, honesty, compassion, or any of the other virtues I was taught as a child?

2. Did I do more good than harm today? Or did I try to? Consider the short term and long-term consequences of your actions.

3. *Did I treat people with dignity and respect today?* All human beings should be treated with dignity simply because they are human. People have moral rights, especially the fundamental right to be treated as free and equal human beings, not as things to be manipulated, controlled, or cast away.

How did my actions today respect the moral rights and the dignified treatment to which every person is entitled?

4. *Was I fair and just today?* Did I treat each person the same unless there was some relevant moral reason to treat him or her differently? Justice requires that we be fair in the way we distribute benefits and burdens. Whom did I benefit and whom did I burden? How did I decide?

5. *Was my community better because I was in it?* Was I better because I was in my community? Consider your primary community; however you define it—as your neighborhood, apartment building, family, company, church, etc. Now ask yourself, was I able to get beyond my own interests to make that community stronger? Was I able to draw on my community's strengths to help me in my own process of becoming more human?

This everyday ethical reflection must occur before we can effectively confront the larger moral questions. A person who wants to take moral leadership on global issues must, according to author Parker Palmer, "take special responsibility for what's going on inside his or her own self, inside his or her own consciousness, lest the act of leadership create more harm than good."

Palmer goes on to suggest that all of us can be leaders for good; the choice is ours. We share a responsibility for creating the external world by projecting either a spirit of light or a spirit of shadow on that which is other than us. We project either a spirit of hope or a spirit of despair.... We have a choice about what we are going to project, and in that choice we help create the world that is.

9

BIBLICAL DISCIPLINE

"To love humanity is easy. The difficulty is to love our neighbor."
—Henry Fonda

One's personal opinion may not always apply, but a biblical principle is lasting. A spiritual leader needs to know biblical principles, for he/she is responsible for the attitude of the church committee.

If we make mistakes when nominating a church member for office because we do not follow the counsel of Matthew 18, imagine what can happen in the even more serious event than the church committee needs to consider the discipline of a member. Even in the case of ecclesiastical discipline, no matter what the reason for the discipline, the biblical principle needs to be applied. The leader who wants to implement the biblical model in church administration needs to apply it in the area of human relations too.

What is the reason for church discipline? Church discipline is a term rarely used in the current Christian vocabulary. With post-modernism, any concept that threatens individualism and freedom of choice, as far as lifestyle and behavior is concerned, is often considered archaic. The fear of unpopularity leads many church leaders to compromise, and sins are justified in the name of a more "humane" attitude. On the other hand, what about those who, in the name of zeal for discipline, commit injustices and cause more harm than good? And what happens to a church with no discipline?

THE CHURCH AND DISCIPLINE

The word "discipline" has several meanings. We may use it to refer to an area of instruction, to the exercise of order, the exercise of piety, or to corrective measures at the heart of the church.[1]

Christian churches have been accused of being the only army that shoots its wounded.[2] The degree of truth in this accusation is often due to misunderstandings related to the ecclesiastical discipline. Such misunderstandings are held by at least two groups: the ones who apply the discipline and the ones who suffer it.

First, we need to remember that every sinful attitude needs to be corrected, but some of them require public correction. For instance, Matthew 18:16-17 talks about those who refuse to abandon sin even after a personal, loving admonition. In 1 Corinthians 5:1-13, Paul describes people whose practices bring scandal to the church, and in 1 Timothy 1:20, 2 Timothy 2:17-18 and 2 John 9-11 are mentioned those who spread teachings contrary to the Gospel. On the other hand, in Romans 16:17 the apostle recommends discipline to those who cause division in the church, and as he writes his second letter to the Thessalonians, in chapter 3:6-10 he prescribes ecclesiastical discipline for those who live in idleness. There is a distinct principle: the sins which were explicitly disciplined in the New Testament were known publicly and were externally evident, and many of them had been practiced for a period of time.[3]

> "Because the Lord disciplines those he loves, and he punishes everyone he accepts as a son."
>
> —Hebrews 12:6

The One who ordains discipline in the church is the same One who establishes the pattern to be followed when exercising it. This pattern reveals paternal love (Hebrews 12:4-13). It is true that the world sees discipline as an expression of anger and hostility, but Scriptures show that God's discipline is the exercise of His love for His children. Love and discipline possess a vital connection (Revelations 3:19). Besides, discipline involves family relationship (Hebrews 12:7-9), and when Christians receive divine discipline, the Heavenly Father is only treating them as His children.

The divine discipline pattern also reveals wonderful benefits. The discipline that comes from the Lord is "for our good" (verse 10). However painful it may seem in the beginning, to receive discipline produces peace and righteousness (verse 11). And verse 13 teaches us that God's purpose in disciplining is not to disable sinners permanently, but to return them to spiritual health.

According to the Scriptures, church discipline is based not only on the exercise of good sense, but primarily on the Lord's imperatives. The biblical mandate regarding discipline is found especially in the teachings of Jesus (Mathews 18:15-17) and in the writings of Paul (I Corinthians 5:1-13). There is also clear biblical reference that the church that neglects the exercise of this mandate compromises not only its spiritual effectiveness but its own existence. A church without discipline is a church without purity (Ephesians 5:25-27) and without power (Joshua 7:11-12a). As an example, I mention the church of Thyatira which was reprimanded due to its tolerance of immorality (Revelation 2:20-24).

Biblically, discipline in the church has a three-point goal:

1. To restore the sinner (Matthew 18:15; 1 Corinthians. 5:5 and Galatians 6:1)
2. To maintain the church's purity (1 Corinthians. 5:6-8)
3. To dissuade others from doing the same (1 Timothy 5:20)

It is this triple goal that suggests the steps to be followed in the application of ecclesiastical discipline. These steps are mentioned in Matthew 18:15-17. In some places, however, this goal has not been reached. Where would the problem be? Would it be in the biblical principle or in those who apply the church discipline?

INDIVIDUAL APPROACH (VERSE 15)

"*If your brother sins against you, go and show him his fault, just between the two of you*" (Mathew 18:15). This verse teaches us that rebuking is a Christian task. One of the best things to be done for a brother in sin is to rebuke him in love (Proverbs 27:5-6). There will always be risks when rebuking someone, for one can never foresee his or her reaction. Jesus, however, leads our attention to the possibility that such a person will listen to us. Besides, the Greek term "legcon" ("interrogate, instruct, rebuke" verse 15) may also be translated as "bring to light, expose."[4]

It is significant that this is the same word used in John 16:8 to describe the Holy Spirit's ministry in relation to those who are in the world, in rebuking them (reproving them) concerning "sin, righteousness and judgment." Thus, before rebuking a brother, we can always cry out for help to the One whose ministry of rebuking is ever effective.

PRIVATE ADMONITION (VERSE 16)

In case the offender does not give heed to the individual who gives the rebuke, Jesus ordains that there should be a less private (one or two elders) and, if necessary, even a public (the whole church) admonition (verse 16). In that case, a greater number of people are involved. At first, it may seem that the purpose of this measure is to intimidate the offender. A deeper understanding, however, leads us to see that its purpose might be to make the offender aware of the damage of his or her attitude to the community of Christ's body. In other words, our sin brings double consequences: individual and collective. Besides, Jesus affirms that the others involved in this process will be witnesses. This is a reference to the Old Testament practice of not condemning anyone based only in one person's opinion (see Numbers 35:30, Deuteronomy 17:6 and 19:15). With that, the objectivity of the case is preserved, which reduces the chance of injustice, and the offender benefits from it.

PUBLIC ANNOUNCEMENT (VERSE 17)

A public announcement of discipline is never a violation of secrets, for the offender has deliberately refused the previous opportunity for repentance. When such an announcement is to be made, each member of the body of Christ should pray for the sinner, avoid needless comments (2 Thessalonians 3:14-15), and keep watch over themselves (1 Corinthians 10:12).[5]

PUBLIC REMOVAL

The last resource in church discipline is removal from the church, historically known as excommunication (from Latin *ex*, "out", and *communicare*, "communicate"), in which the offender was deprived of all benefits of communion. The offender was considered a gentile (who was not allowed to enter the sacred chambers of the Lord's temple) and publican (considered a traitor and apostate: Luke 19:2-10). There was no longer Christian communion with them, for they had deliberately refused the principles of Christian life (1 Corinthians 5:11). The Seventh-day Adventist church has chosen the "disfellowship" terminology instead of excommunication.

The church today has a concept more redemptive than punitive. I believe that discipline is a loving plan from God to restore His children. The Bible says, "Because the LORD disciplines those he loves, as a father the son he delights in" (Proverbs 3:12). The *Church Manual,* in chapter 14, page 194 comments: "Removing an individual from membership in the church, the body of Christ, is always a serious matter; it is the ultimate in the discipline that the church can administer; it is the extreme measure that can be meted out by the church. *Only after the instruction given in this chapter has been followed and after all possible efforts have made to win and restore him/her to right paths,* should this kind of discipline be used."

Of course, in each of the steps that involve ecclesiastical discipline, there is a job to be done, before, during, and afterwards. In that sense, nothing should be done without prayer, visitation, and love. Many times this process is accompanied by sadness and hurt. It is not pleasant. There is, however, the comfort of knowing that the presence and power of Jesus are real, even in the context of this process (Matthew 18:19-20). Thus, ecclesiastical discipline is not an activity easily performed, but rather, something to be conducted in close relationship with the Lord.

Considering that Christ desires His church to be "without stain or wrinkle or any other blemish, but holy and blameless" (Ephesians 5:27), ecclesiastical discipline is highly relevant, for it is God's way of keeping His church pure.

REBELLION AGAINST GOD'S AUTHORITY

Sinful humans are naturally rebellions against authority. This is a consequence of Satan's original rebellion against God's righteous rule. Today we see as never before rebellion against authority in the home, school, government, and church.

If the church neglects Scriptural teachings concerning church discipline, we are simply condoning a devilish, independent spirit and cooperating in rebellion against God's authority. The fact that we prefer our ways and will to God's way and God's will underlies the problem. God expects us to behave differently because He has saved us. More importantly, God expects us to treat others, especially those we term sinners, differently because He has saved us. Of course, He expects us to submit to His authority. He also expects us to follow His example.

FOLLOWING JESUS' EXAMPLE IN CHURCH DISCIPLINE

When Paul wrote to the brethren at the church of Corinth, he reminded them that to neglect dealing with the case of immorality in their midst would affect the whole congregation (1 Corinthians 5:6-8). Discipline is necessary. But notice how Jesus dealt with a similar situation in the story of the woman "taken in adultery." Especially note their wrong approach when her accusers attempted to deal *only with the adulterous woman* while ignoring the sin of the man who clearly had led her into the sinful situation.

Of course, to ignore sin that should be dealt with in our local congregations makes it appear to others that the church condones it. But it is equally disastrous if we fail to follow Jesus' gracious example in our treatment of sinners. When Jesus dealt with the adulterous woman, His first enquiry was, "Where are your accusers?" Her accusers had disappeared under the conviction of their own sinful motivations, and their hate-filled judgmentalism had also evaporated.

Next Jesus stated, "Neither do I condemn you." This is not cheap grace. Jesus was not letting her off the "spiritual hook," nor was he minimizing her spiritual jeopardy. His final response clearly shows this: "Go and sin no more!"

THE GOSPEL ENVISIONS
THE SPIRITUAL IMPACT OF DISCIPLINE.

Jesus demonstrated the importance of a standard when he told His listeners, "Not only should you avoid adultery; you shouldn't even permit evil fantasizing which also breaks the commandment." But when He dealt with the sinner, herself, He refused the course of retribution; He did not initiate the required penalty of death by stoning. Instead, He demonstrated that a loving, forgiving experience will often transform sinners into saints.

That's what it means to be transformed by love!

Churches may neglect the practice of church discipline because they fear displeasing the people. However, redemptive discipline pleases God and, ultimately, it will please the members because the Holy Spirit's transforming power enables them to view sinners as Jesus views sinners—candidates for His kingdom.

Of course, there are times when a situation is so grievous that action must be taken to protect the innocent victims of those who use their power and influence to prey upon others. Predatory abuse and violence can never be condoned and must be excised as thoroughly as a physician would surgically remove a cancerous tumor.

But when you preach the Gospel, make certain to tell people who feel hopelessly lost that they can be born again and washed in the blood of Christ. This is the gospel!

J. Carl Laney admonishes us saying, "Discipline is like a strong medication: it can bring healing or cause greater damage."[6] No medical professional, however, refuses to apply a medication that could cure a patient simply because it is strong. Neither will someone who is ill choose to die or to remain ill if life and a cure may be near.

Serious reflection about the counsel on ecclesiastical discipline makes evident two basic principles. First, church discipline is not an option, but rather an ordinance, and consequently, a divine blessing (Hebrews 12:5-7). Second, discipline requires deep love from the church applying it, and equal humility and brokenness of heart from the one who is being disciplined (2 Corinthians 2:5-11).

Even when one is disciplining, the name and reputation of the church member should be preserved. This needs to be practiced as a commandment, for it is part of the biblical instruction that we as a church and as spiritual leaders receive from God.

---

[1] Richard J. Foster, *Celebration of Discipline: The Paths to Spiritual Growth* (HarperCollins, 1998).

[2] Carl J. Laney, "The Biblical Practice of Church Discipline," *Bibliotheca Sacra* 143 (October-December 1986) pp. 353-64.

[3] Wayne Grudem, *Systematic Theology* (Grand Rapids: Zondervan, 1994), p. 896. The only exception to this principle was the secret sin of Ananias and Sapphira (Acts 5:1-11). In that sense, the extraordinary action of the Holy Spirit caused great fear among church members.

[4] F. F. Bruce, ed., *Vine's Expository Dictionary of Old and New Testament Words* (Fleming H. Revell, 1981), pp. 283-4.

[5] R. N. Caswell, "Discipline," in the *New Dictionary of Theology*, eds. S. B. Ferguson, D. F. Wright, and J. I. Packer (Downers Grove: InterVarsity, 1988), p. 200.

[6] Carl J. Laney, "The Biblical Practice of Church Discipline," p. 363.

10

THE IMPORTANCE OF CONVICTION AND CONFIDENTIALITY

"Blessed is the leader who seeks the best for those he serves."
—*Unknown*

I like to make things as practical as possible. As leaders we have to develop personal guidelines for church work. Not everything is written down in a manual regarding every detail of the decisions we make and procedures we follow. But there is a key principle: People are more important than anything else. Even in the most serious cases of ecclesiastical discipline, it is up to us to preserve the good name and reputation of church members. Is that possible?

One day I was told that a member of my church had had an intimate relationship with a non-Christian young lady and that she was pregnant. As soon as I heard the news, I tried to contact him. I was invited to his house for a more personal talk. When I met him, there was no need to ask if the information was true, for his face clearly revealed something was very wrong. Without my having to ask anything, he quickly went right to the subject and confirmed it. Everything was true.

I could see he was deeply sorry and ashamed for what had happened. He confessed that it was foolish, something he had never done before. Now, as a married man, he didn't know how to face his wife and two small children. He was convinced of his mistake.

Without conviction, men would never be ready to admit their sins. Conviction prepares for repentance. Sorrow, according to God (2 Corinthians 7:10) precedes repentance, which is a permanent change of the sinner's heart and mind. Although conviction is the Holy Spirit's job, He is pleased to use certain truths, such as:

• **The Law** (Romans 3:19-20; 7:7-13). Men usually judge themselves by their neighbors' actions, but through conviction they understand that the glory of God is what they lack (Romans 3:23).

• **God's Grace and Kindness** (Romans 2:4). Many people have testified that it was their understanding of God's kindness that convinced them of their sins.

THE MARKS OF TRUE CONVICTION

Ellen G. White says, "The Holy Spirit is not only to sanctify but to convict. No one can repent of his sins until he is convicted of his guilt. How necessary, then, it is that we should have the Holy Spirit with us as we labor to reach fallen souls. Our human abilities will be exercised in vain unless they are united with this heavenly agency."[1] She also says, "In His great mercy, God has spoken words of encouragement to the children of men. To all who repent and turn to Him, He offers abundant pardon. Repentance for sin is the first fruits of the working of the Holy Spirit in the life."[2]

True conviction makes men accept their fault (Psalm 51:4; Luke 18:9-14), it destroys selfishness (Luke 18:9-14; Isaiah 64:6), makes them see sin as being against God (Psalm 51:4; Luke 15:18), and also leads them to Christ, not to despair (2 Corinthians 7:10).

Conviction may not be a pleasant work, but it is needed. In the first four blessings (Matthew 5:3-6) Jesus explains that only those who know and experience true conviction are really blessed.

I could see in the eyes of the man I visited the anguish, suffering and disillusion caused by his sin. I beheld in his eyes the despair of a husband, father and Christian who did not know where to run or hide himself. I tried to encourage him, saying that I would help him spiritually, but that at that moment I would have to manage things the ecclesiastical way, for in some aspects the church was involved. As a strategy to minimize the dishonor

> "Conviction is worthless unless it is converted into conduct."
>
> —*Thomas Carlyle*

73

that the whole situation would eventually cause, I asked him to write a letter to the Church Committee, asking them to remove his name from the membership rolls, for personal reasons. He immediately accepted the suggestion and prepared a letter, trusting that as his church's spiritual leader I would do for him the best I could.

TRUST AND CREDIBILITY

As spiritual leaders, many times we have failed in matters that require confidentiality or secrecy. As a result, there is a credibility crisis within church leadership. Unpleasant facts that occurred in the past lead members to no longer trust their leaders. To restore that credibility is an imperative and an urgent need that requires a commitment from everyone.

Confidentiality is a critical issue in our churches today. When confidences are broken, relational, emotional, vocational, and even spiritual damage is likely to follow. Sadly, often the greatest offenses of breaking confidences happen among well-intentioned people who have a heart to help. Those involved in a helping ministry include pastors, elders, ministry team leaders, all group leaders, and others who function in similar roles. The helping relationship occurs when one person turns to another for help in personal matters. Unless specific permission is given, the personal information shared is presumed confidential.

A helping ministry will succeed only in an atmosphere of trust between church, helper, and the one helped. The one helped will trust the helper only when he/she knows that the information he/she shares with the helper will be held in strict confidence. The church will trust a helper only when it knows he/she will act appropriately to protect the body of Christ from harm.

If you can't trust your pastor to keep a secret, who can you trust? Suppose you went to your pastor and confessed a continuing problem of shoplifting or adultery. You sought his prayers and counsel. You prayed with him for God's forgiveness and strength to renew your life. But alas, the problem continued; you tired of the pastor's assistance and spoke no further with him about it. Then suppose you found out he had told the deacons about your problem. Or imagine he told you that unless you changed your conduct, he would "tell it to the church." What would your reaction be?

What if you were the pastor? What would you do? Would you advise other church leaders and follow step two of Matthew 18? Would you eventually "tell it to the church"? Or is the information confidential?

Or suppose the counseling ministry of your church is ministering to a church member who acknowledges a drug problem that is affecting her life and marriage. She has been nominated by the church for a position of leadership. As a counselor, what should you do with this information morally, biblically, and legally?

Most of us expect that if we acknowledge a transgression or identify a problem to our pastor, it is personal and not intended to be shared with others. Indeed, most of us would be quite surprised and angry to hear our story become the sermon illustration on Sabbath or used as a church discipline example for the elders. When we seek spiritual help with a problem, we

> "Confidentiality is a virtue of the loyal, as loyalty is the virtue of faithfulness."
>
> —*Edwin Louis Cole*

do not expect it to become public information. Yet when the counseling is proving ineffective and the ongoing conduct is serious and destructive, there are biblical expectations that seem to run against absolute secrecy. From a purely spiritual perspective, what we wish to keep hidden and secret may need to be brought into the light.

THE SIGNIFICANCE OF CONFIDENTIALITY

Confidentiality is a requirement by no means unique to the pastorate. Nor is it always more crucial to the pastorate than to other professions. Doctors and hospitals who deal with the sick must keep many medical secrets. Lawyers and those in law enforcement dealing daily with laws and crime must keep their legal secrets. Bankers and businessmen have their financial secrets, journalists their news sources, politicians and soldiers their snares and strategies, writers and composers their original creations, and so forth. Not one of these professions could function without honoring secrets.

Within every family and individual, there are private matters—sins, aspirations, hopes, suspicions, and so forth—never to be revealed at large without causing the breakdown of personal trust and relationship among people, so that, indeed, all society relies on the judicious practice of confidentiality. This by no means belittles the significance of confidentiality for the pastorate and eldership. Clergy deal daily with sinners, and therefore have much to conceal, for "there is not a righteous man on earth who does what is right and never sins" (Ecclesiastes 7:20).

WHEN CONFIDENTIALITY MUST BE BROKEN

There are times when the gray area becomes black and white. In such a situation, swift action must be taken. For instance, if you're certain that a student has moved beyond experimentation and is using an illegal drug regularly or engaging in the sale of drugs, parents should be notified. In this situation, depending on your relationship with the student, you may want to let him know you're going to the parents, especially if he'll likely find out anyway. Or you could offer him 24 hours to tell his parents himself, or invite him to go with you.

If a student is talking seriously about taking their own life, it's also time for action. Remember that parents will always forgive you for erring on the side of caution.

In the case of a child whom you know or strongly suspect is being abused by his parents, huddle with a trusted church leader who can help you report it. Defending the defenseless must be a priority.

Unfortunately, there are few hard and fast rules. Crisis situations are complicated and must be navigated with prayer, wisdom, and the help of trusted advisers.

When we lose the members' trust, we lose our qualification and credibility to continue serving as leaders. Trust and credibility generate qualification and respect in the exercise of leadership.

Some tips for church leaders

Abuse is neither gender nor age specific but the vast majority of those abused are women and children. Statistics reflect that 95% of domestic violence victims are women, although men may also be victims. But regardless of who is victimized, domestic violence is a serious problem that needs to be addressed by religious communities.[3]

A church leader can:

- Recognize that abuse happens even in your church.
- Do all to ensure that your church is a safe place for all.
- Make your church a comfortable and safe place, free of abuse.
- Respect confidentiality.

- Be a good listener in order to validate the pain and brokenness of victims.
- Withhold judgment while supporting the victims and the entire family.
- Know what community support is available in order to refer people as appropriate.
- Have information regarding abuse available to your congregations.
- When possible and as appropriate, support local women's shelters.
- Address issues on abuse from the pulpit.
- Hold perpetrators accountable for their actions.
- Reaffirm the worth of all people.
- Be aware of the barriers victims face.
- Encourage members to talk about abuse.
- Know your limitations in dealing with abuse issues and cases.
- Assist/arrange for the safety and support of victims.

Don't:
- Use religious teachings and sermons to support abuse.
- Forget that the safety of the victim is most important.
- Deny and minimize violence.
- Ignore, cover, deny or remain silent about abuse.
- Breach the confidentiality of the victim.
- Allow excuses for family violence.
- Assume a role for which you were not trained.[4]

CONFIDENTIALITY IN MY CHURCH

At the church committee meeting we had described earlier, among the many items in the agenda I included the letter with brother Alberto's request (fictitious name). I presented the fact that I had received a letter from him asking to have his name removed from the roll of church members for personal reasons. Once the proposal was presented, I asked if I had a motion to discuss the matter. Some hands were raised. I asked if there were any observations. Someone asked, "Pastor, could you tell the committee the real motive for brother Alberto's request?" I immediately said I could and that the real motive was expressed in the letter: "personal reasons." He quickly replied, "Pastor, I have experience in church committees, and I'm old enough to be your father. There must certainly be a reason for this request?" With a lot of serenity, love and assurance I said that if there was a different motive he should look for it some place else. I reaffirmed that in the committee the "motive was personal."

Usually in church committees we have some members who are quite extreme in their attitudes. And that is a problem, for they are usually not familiar with the ethical and biblical principles regarding ecclesiastical discipline. In some cases these people are honest in their intention, but honesty without knowledge and wisdom is dangerous, because it may cause damage beyond repair.

---

[1] Ellen G. White. "The great need of the Holy Spirit." *The Review and Herald*, July 16, 1895.

[2] Ellen G. White, *Sermons and Talks*, Volume 1 (1990), p. 389.

[3] FaithTrust Institute. "Working together to end sexual & domestic violence." Brochure, rev. 01/05.

[4] Amelia Rose, "A Minister's Guide to Understanding Domestic Violence."

11

A MODERATE APPROACH
TO DISCIPLINE

"Unity is a vital and even existential characteristic of the church.
All who foment disunity are involved in a questionable
and perhaps destructive activity. The trademark of arrogance
is presuming I'm right and everybody else is wrong."
—*Anonymous*

Fanaticism and radicalism are problems Christians have had to face in all ages. As a result, this has delayed the proclamation of the Gospel, caused disunity among Christians, and depreciated the image of Christianity before the world. Unfortunately, good Christians at times mistake radicalism or fanaticism for spiritual zeal. The line between them may seem tenuous, but they are not hard to distinguish. There are certain characteristics that fanatics possess which might help us to better identify and deal with them:

• **Fanatics usually reveal a certain inability to keep a sense of proportion in their beliefs and practices.**

When they are impressed with a message, their minds soon are dominated by that subject. They talk about that subject all the time. They summarize their Christian life to that point. They also lose the spiritual vision and the sense of proportion. The situation is aggravated when they concentrate on an insignificant case while important matters of faith become obscured.

- **Fanatics seek to make everyone in the church agree with their point of view.**

It is natural for them to do it. They believe their point of view is of great importance; why shouldn't they seek to make everyone else think the same way? The problem here is not so much the fervor, but the motives that instigate such fervor.

- **Fanatics almost always condemn those who refuse to accept their line of thought.**

When fervor heats up to the point that there is intolerance, the most dangerous effects of fanaticism are seen. Fanatics, in most cases, are incapable of seeing that those who refuse to agree with them are doing it based on common sense and with intellectual and spiritual honesty.

- **In general, when church members refuse to accept the fanatic's point of view, the fanatic begins to criticize the church and the entire Adventist movement.**

When this critical disposition is developed, fanatics feel the church is so far from the right path that they should depart from it. But while they are still in the church, they have the ability to pull others away from the church.

- **Despite their fervor and zeal, fanatics hardly ever accomplish any great good.**

When their effects are evaluated over time, one notes that fanatics provide the church nothing constructive but rather a spirit of division, criticism and doubt.

- **Most fanatics seem to contaminate themselves with subtle heresies.**

It is very easy for all of us to think that if we follow a specific program or accomplish certain things we will become holy and just before God. Such heresy is shown, many times, in the emphasis some give to the doctrine of health reform. We cannot assure holiness by what we eat or don't eat. Some, who follow the health principles, seem to promote that doctrine. However, it should be noted that obedience to the laws of our physical being is related to our spiritual as well as our physical health.

- **Fanatics and radicals are usually distinguished by their spiritual pride.**

Pride reveals itself in different ways. It may come disguised in the form of fervor for God. However, it is nothing but spiritual pride when finite beings, without any natural gifts, sit in judgment of church members who disagree with their ideas.[1]

Referring again to our story of the church committee, we find that they finally recommended the removal of brother Alberto's name without major problems or comments.

Six months later Alberto's extra-marital affair became known. The church brethren sought me, worried, expressing concern, and asking what the church was going to do with him. It's interesting to know that some members are always more ready to judge than to express mercy for the restoration of a hurt brother. My answer was quick: NOTHING! And I justified it by saying it was not up to the church to judge someone who was no longer a member. Therefore, it was not up to the members to make any comments or observations about the case.

Important advice: The *Church Manual* recommends that when someone asks to have his/her name taken off the church roll, it is up to the church committee to accept or reject the request, without making any comments: "Although we recognize the right of an individual to decide whether or not to belong to the church, ample time should be given such a member for sober thought and reflection, and every effort made to restore this individual to a satisfactory experience. The letters of resignation should be presented to the church board, which will forward them to the church at a duly called business meeting. Out of Christian consideration for the individuals involved, action shall be taken without public discussion."[2] What the *Church Manual* is trying to say is: "It is forbidden to gossip."

On the other hand, when the case is made public and it is known by most members, to request a letter asking to remove an individual's name from the roll of members for personal reasons would not be the best procedure. In that case, because the matter is known, the subject should not be solved in a private manner. However, if the person by his/her own initiative asks to have their name removed for personal reasons before the church committee meets, thus avoiding any discussion regarding their lack of ethics, it is up to the committee to accept or reject the request. This may also help to avoid damage caused by the process of ecclesiastical discipline. But when nothing is done by the erring member, the committee should be summoned to wisely discuss the problem presented.

> "The virtue of justice consists in moderation, as regulated by wisdom."
>
> —*Aristotle*

SAYING ONLY WHAT IS NECESSARY

In such a case, to avoid any risks—and be assured that everyone knows what has happened—it would be wise to ask the church committee members if they are aware of what happened to brother Alberto. Even if everyone says *yes,* it would be wise for the leader to clarify what happened, without entering into details or saying too much. Remember that even when someone's problem is made public, we should preserve the image and reputation of those involved. Ellen G. White counsels, "Let the shepherds have a tender care for the flock of the Lord's pasture. Let them speak to the erring of the forgiving mercy of the Saviour. Let them encourage the sinner to repent, and believe in Him who can pardon."[3] We might say: "As you know, unfortunately brother Alberto was unfaithful to his wife. We have already visited him, and he is deeply repentant. As spiritual leaders, we have a job to do in his behalf. However, according to the *Church Manual,* this moral fault requires a removal discipline. Does anyone propose this ecclesiastical discipline? It is proposed. Any comments?"

I remember that once, as we were dealing with a similar case, someone in the committee raised his hand and asked: "Pastor, could you give us more details?" I usually ask, "What kind of details do you want?" That person then went on, asking: "Did it occur at a hotel or at home? Were there any mirrors on the ceiling?" It is absurd to ask such questions which are no help whatsoever in solving the problem. If we cannot avoid this type of comment or observation, we should at least say that it does not help; on the contrary, it only serves to damage the person's image even more. Ellen G. White advises the church members, "They should not even express their prejudices regarding the erring; for thus they place in other minds the leaven of evil."[4]

Unfortunately, sometimes we have to deal with hard-hearted and insensitive people at committee meetings. Some of them are not satisfied until they see the sinner's blood running down the aisle. At times, a type of inquisition has been allowed. This does not fulfill the divine purpose regarding ecclesiastical discipline. Ellen G. White affirms that "Church-members have no right to follow their own impulses and inclinations in dealing with fellow-members who have erred."[5]

DON'T BE TOO HASTY

Some church officers are always in a hurry to discipline, and forget to follow the steps that precede ecclesiastical discipline. One of the wisest attitudes is to wait for the right moment. The urge to resolve a situation or problem quickly may lead us to haste and imprudence. On the other hand, if we wait too long, we might lose the most appropriate opportunity. How do we know the right moment?

First of all, we must remember not to make an important decision when we are emotionally involved. Rage, passion, hurt, pride, or conceit may lead us to make decisions in the heat of the moment. These decisions are usually dangerous, for we are not rational, and our ability to analyze the situation may be—and usually is—deeply affected by our emotions. Ellen G. White counsels: "Do not suffer sin upon your brother; but do not expose him, and thus increase the difficulty, making the reproof seem like a revenge. Correct him in the way outlined in the word of God."[6]

One time, as I was transferred to a new church, in my first meeting with the church committee members an elder raised his hand and said: "Pastor, we were expecting your arrival, for we have many matters to discuss, including a case of discipline to consider, and we cannot wait one more day." The only question I asked was whether anyone had visited the person who was being disciplined. I could see that no one had visited the person, but some were anxious to act and they hastened to apply discipline. Ellen G. White affirms: "No church officer should advise, no committee should recommend, nor should any church vote, that the name of a wrong-doer shall be removed from the church books, until the instruction given by Christ has been faithfully followed. When this has been done, the church has cleared herself before God."[7]

"Moderation is the inseparable companion of wisdom, but with it genius has not even a nodding acquaintance."

—*Charles Caleb Colton*

Part of the instruction given by Christ is related to a visit to the member at fault. Yet I have met people who were removed from the church roll without having received a visit or any communication about the church's decision. That is unconscionable. In a situation like that, those who should suffer ecclesiastical discipline are the committee members, for not following the counsel given in the Bible and in the Spirit of Prophecy.

When the church members hear about certain thoughtless attitudes by the church committee, they automatically ask themselves: How can the church, as a divine institution, display so much harshness? How can the church preach the peace of Jesus Christ while people inside its ranks are often fighting? How can the church preach Christian ethics based in the kingdom of God while members are ignoring ethical principles?

A TASK FOR EVERYONE

We all are responsible for the image of the church. Each one has to fulfill his/her part in the body of Christ so that the whole may be blessed. It would be good if we criticize the church less and spent that same time praying for it. Take this as a mission to be accomplished.

Ellen G. White affirms: "The church is God's appointed agency for the salvation of men. It was organized for service, and its mission is to carry the gospel to the world. From the beginning it has been God's plan that through His church shall be reflected to the world His fullness and His sufficiency. The members of the church, those whom He has called out of darkness into His marvelous light, are to show forth His glory. The church is the repository of the riches of the grace of Christ; and through the church will eventually be made manifest, even to 'the principalities and powers in heavenly places,' the final and full display of the love of God" (Ephesians 3:10).[8]

---

[1] Luiz Marins, *Anthropos Motivação & Sucesso,* a newsletter (adapted, modified and amplified by the author of the book).

[2] *Church Manual*, General Conference of Seventh-day Adventists, (Review and Herald, 2005) chapter 14.

[3] Ellen G. White, *Gospel Workers*, p. 503.

[4] *Ibid*, 498.

[5] *Ibid*.

[6] *Ibid*.

[7] *Ibid.*, 501

[8] Ellen G. White, *Acts of the Apostles*, p. 9.

12

DOING WHAT IS RIGHT
IN THE RIGHT WAY

"Next to doing the right thing, the most important thing is to let people know you are doing the right thing."
—John D. Rockefeller

A positive church is always interested in doing the right thing the right way. In ecclesiastical disciplinary cases, it is important to be aware that we are dealing with people who are spiritually and emotionally hurting. They will be sensitive to any kind of comment or observation. Thus, one should be very aware of their feelings, taking care not to increase their suffering. We do not have the right to make anyone suffer, even if our intention is to help restore them.

When we discipline someone, the recommendation usually comes from the committee. However, because the committee does not have the final word, the final decision is up to the church in a properly called meeting. In many churches, the reading of the Church Committee minutes is done on a Sabbath morning, between Sabbath School and Worship Service, or at the end of the program.

But have we ever considered whether Sabbath is the best day to enforce ecclesiastical discipline? Would this be the best day for the committee to meet and discipline a member of their family? Yet many churches conduct this activity on the Sabbath. Some may defend this practice, believing there is no problem in using the Sabbath hours for such procedures, since discipline should be a blessing, providing for the spiritual good of the erring member.

However, let's illustrate this. Do you believe that because of Adam and Eve's sin, God expelled them from the Garden between the heavenly Sabbath School and the subsequent Worship service? It seems more likely that God would have done it on a different day of the week, at a better moment for such discipline. Sabbath is a day for celebration, fellowship, joy, union and worship. A day of blessing! As a spiritual leader, would you have the courage to ruin the Sabbath atmosphere of your church by administering ecclesiastical discipline on this day?

For many years this has been the practice. When the question is raised: "Why do you make this decision on Sabbath?" The answer is often: "Everybody does that. I learned it by seeing others doing it." This reminds me of the old expression of "the cow's path." Some have followed that trail in the past, others continue to follow it, and perhaps many will continue to follow the same trail in the future without asking, "Is this the best way?"

Others may suggest it is done on Sabbath because most church members are together on Sabbath. However, according to the *Church Manual,* having a majority of the congregation present was never a prerequisite to discipline someone. The *Church Manual* does not require the vote of the majority of the church members, but merely the vote of the majority of members present in a properly called meeting.

> "Efficiency is
> doing things right;
> effectiveness is doing
> the right things."
>
> —Peter Drucker

Older members might recall that in the past a church committee meeting was reason for dread and fear. It was often a kind of judgment that was being held. Why has such a negative image been created? Why do so many today still hold on to that concept?

One important lesson to learn is that Sabbath should *not* be used for Church Committee meetings. It is definitely not the best day for such work. Many subjects to be discussed are important church business but have nothing to do with the spirit of the Sabbath.

A second lesson is that Sabbath is not the appropriate day for disciplining members. Keep in mind, and help your church members remember, that Sabbath is a special day, a holy day. Every disciplinary action, even the ones made within a Christian ethical context, generates pain and sadness. Therefore, do not use the Sabbath hours for this purpose. Choose a different day.

In many countries the Adventist Church meets on Sundays for evangelistic meetings. In others, churches also meet on Wednesdays for prayer meetings. Some churches are more creative, revolutionizing the paradigm and having worship services every day of the week. They are having beautiful experiences and receiving great blessings.

Perhaps one of the best times for consideration of ecclesiastical discipline is when we are gathered for prayer meeting. The purpose and environment is different. Talking about redemption, restoration, and forgiveness with a group gathered for prayer would surely be more appropriate.

A BAD CHURCH TRADITION

I remember an unfortunate incident that occurred when I was young. When the time during the service arrived to care for a disciplinary matter, the pastor asked the visitors to leave, announcing that only church members should remain. After the visitors left, he asked the deacons to lock the church doors so that no one could walk out and no visitors could listen to the discussion.

I can only imagine what my reaction would be if I were a church member who had brought a visitor to church that morning for the first time. Should I go out with my friend, or stay and fulfill my role as an active member? What should I do? Do I leave, or do I say to my friend, "Please, wait outside for 30 minutes. As soon as this meeting is over, I'll meet you there." Just imagine the confusion that would create in a visitor's mind. Imagine the guest slowly going out, with questions: "Why do I have to leave? What are they going to say that I shouldn't hear? Are they going to talk about me?" I imagine my friend waiting outside, for 10 minutes, 30 minutes, or even one hour, until the church door is finally reopened and worshipers emerge.

He quickly notices people's faces. The happy expressions he saw during the closing hymn and prayer have disappeared. Some look sad, others are crying, and others walk out quickly. My friend might ask, "What happened?"

"Oh, you can't imagine!" Someone might answer. "We just cut off a member. A church member has committed adultery and the church had to disfellowship him. I realize he deserved this discipline, for it was a huge sin."

At these moments we run the risk of passing on a negative message regarding the church as we don't effectively share what happened with appropriate words. The conclusion visitors might make is that if one day they become church members, they will certainly not be attending that congregation, and they will probably never come back to visit.

In my experience as a pastor, I've decided not to ask the visitors to leave anymore. I've decided to adopt a more clear and teachable attitude—an attitude that is certainly more ethical and balanced. I know, however, that a decision for discipline involves the participation of only regular church members.

> **"Tell me what is right and I will fight for it."**
>
> —*Woodrow Wilson*

The procedure I adopted was to announce, after a weekday service—and certainly not on a Sabbath—that the service had ended, but we had a report from the Church Committee to present. I explained that it dealt with discipline of a member, and that visiting friends were free to stay, and it would be a pleasure to have their company a little longer. Then I explained in a few minutes that discipline is part of life. It is present in our daily lives, as a family, at work, at school, in sports, and in many other situations. The church is no different. We have many biblical guidelines on how to proceed in these cases and on how discipline may represent a blessing in the life of a child of God when applied in the biblical way and at the right time.

I explained that, as the pastor, I had already visited the person; that we were spiritually counseling them and that, as a church, we love them very much. I said that the person has repented and will soon be reconciled with the church as a regular member, but for now, with love and sorrow in our hearts, we have to take the step of disciplining them. I usually spend more time preparing the church for the decision than talking about the problem itself. The entire process doesn't take more than 10 minutes.

When I ask, "How many are in favor?" even the visitors raise their hands supporting the discipline. Why does this happen? The reason is because everything is done with transparency and in the right way. Some visitors, impressed by the process even say that if one day they became church members, it would surely be a pleasure to belong to this congregation, for things are done with clarity, love, and mercy.

I remember a pastor, apparently harsh in the way he treated erring members, who disciplined a young man in such an inappropriate way that the mother fainted inside the church and had to receive emergency treatment. What a tragedy! What a poor example! Some, when being disciplined, become so ashamed they never come back to church. I knew a church member who, after being disciplined and having his image destroyed, moved to another town. He never again wanted to see those who in the past had called him a brother in Christ. Unfortunately, some churches support this type of procedure by allowing it.

While I was writing this book, a current example came to me. I received an e-mail from a former member of our church who had recently been removed. I share with you part of the message.

"Regarding my family, everyone is fine, but not attending church. We are still Christians, but it wouldn't be good to go to church with so many doubts in our minds. We are taking some time off, as long as our current pastor is in our church. My son has been cut off from church simply because he was hired to work as a minister of music at a different denomination. I'm not going to discuss their decision right now, but I have been excluded too, in a traumatic way, and neither the pastor nor anyone else from the church committee sought us to deal with the subject as a family. Because of this, my wife is no longer attending church either. We were really trying to forgive these attitudes when one day my children were invited to pay a tribute to my wife (their mother) on mother's day, and one of my sons was intercepted because (according to some LEGALISTS from the church committee conducted by the pastor) he was an apostate and had denied his faith. We thought that was absurd, for above all, I'm a Christian, and I fully believe that Christ would be seeking the lost sheep. In my opinion, the pastor and the church members lack much love. Would this be the end? Why does the church preach one thing and practice another? It makes me very sad to see the church I came to love more concerned with an institution and with denominational rules than with the redemption of its members."

This kind of message brings pain to my heart. As spiritual leaders, our attitude should be more redemptive than merely disciplinary. But the story above is only one example of many.

When people are truly spiritual, their spirituality is manifested in the way they live, serve, and listen to the Lord. Spirituality is measured only by God, not by one's own declarations. A clear sign of spiritual greatness and maturity is a spirit of service, love, and meekness.

AVOIDING OTHER MISTAKES

In many churches, when a matter of discipline is presented to the members, the matter is presented carelessly and without thought. For example, we should never announce that a person who committed adultery is being disciplined for adultery. Remember that it is not by using harsh words or by "calling sin by its name" that you will be restoring and helping these people, but by the way you deal with the case before, during, and after the discipline.

I don't mean to say that sin should be cherished or hidden, but that the sinner should be helped, loved and understood. Always imagine the possibility that it could be your own children.

I met a pastor who, when conducting a disciplinary process in the church, would conclude by saying the members were forbidden to talk to that "sinner" (term he used to describe the person who had been disfellowshipped), for in doing so they would be participants in the same sin. What an absurd idea!

Another thoughtless leader, when presenting the reason for ecclesiastical discipline, announced publicly that it was for ADULTERY. The disciplined member was ashamed before the church, deeply offended, and upset with the pastor and church for the thoughtless way his disciplinary case was conducted. He appealed to a lawyer and explained his case. The lawyer brought a lawsuit against the pastor for moral damage. The judge requested a copy of the Church Committee minutes. The lawyer told the church that the pastor would go to jail or would have to pay a large fine for the inappropriate procedure. Unfortunately, sometimes people who do not understand the difference between being firm and being harsh in implementing their decisions make glaring errors in judgment.

As spiritual leaders we should be careful in the way we treat certain problems that members face. We cannot compromise the name of the church by our thoughtless behavior and our lack of Christian ethics. We do not have the right. We are representatives of the church and of our Lord before the community. We need to represent both well. We must discard personal opinions or habits that do not reflect well on the church.

When the pastor who was threatened with a lawsuit realized he had mishandled the member's disciplinary problem, he requested the assistance of the ministerial secretary of his field. Because it was a new and complicated case, the ministerial secretary requested the assistance of the Union Conference ministerial secretary, who went to that church and held a meeting with the congregation. He explained the mistake the pastor, the church committee, and the members had made (since the final decision on a disciplinary matter, be it conducted in a good or bad way, does not belong to one person, but to the entire church). He suggested that the church cancel the original vote and change its terminology. The church took a new vote. The reason registered now was "deviation from biblical principles." Certainly a more appropriate terminology, much less offensive and wording that did not compromise the image of the church, the pastor, or the disciplined member.

When the lawyer received a copy of the Church Committee minutes with the new reason for the ecclesiastical discipline of his client, he responded that the church had corrected the problem and that they no longer had a basis for a lawsuit against the pastor. The lawyer was extremely kind in this case.

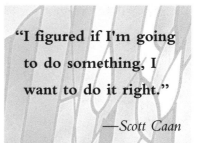

> "I figured if I'm going to do something, I want to do it right."
>
> —*Scott Caan*

Another mistake for local leaders to avoid is overreacting when the church as a whole feels the church committee went beyond what it should. When an inappropriate matter is presented to the church, and the church rejects it, a wise leader will not force the situation to obtain votes. He or she will not use emotional manipulation or make long speeches. It is best to remove the subject from the agenda and discuss it more fully with the committee members. In this way leaders can avoid diminishing their credibility.

You may think of examples of people who suffered injustices in relation to discipline or other ecclesiastical problem. You may have many questions or comments, but because this is a book, you don't have the opportunity to ask me. I may not have all the answers either, so take the opportunity to evaluate the way you, as a spiritual leader of your church, have been working to solve these and other ministerial problems. Stop, reflect, and always try to find new ways and wiser methods for their resolution.

I challenge you to do what is right in the most appropriate way possible, for the church's reputation is in your hands. In a world with so many negatives, the church could be like a "white lily in the midst of mud." It could be the place where justice, hope, comfort, help, and genuine love are practiced by all. It could be like the inscription I saw on a church pulpit, "Pain stops here." Or like the sign at another church's entrance: "Smile, you are being forgiven."

The church as a divine institution should be an example to the world where there is so much injustice. We should never see the world behaving better than the church does. Although the church is imperfect, weak and defective, this does not give us the right to perpetuate mistakes of the past.

Why speak ill if we can speak well? Why continue with old traditions if there are new and better ways? Let us use our creativity to make the church a pleasant place to be. Today you may start a new page in your church's history. Do not wait for the initiative of others. Start yourself, and your attitude will influence others. Why? Because in this world the power of good still reigns over evil.

Therefore, live an uncommon life in a world where everything may seem common, because one day what is common will end, and what is uncommon will be common for all eternity.

13

YOUR GOOD NAME IS SAFE IN OUR HOUSE

"There are those among us who would recoil in horror at the thought of stealing another person's money or property but who don't give a second thought to stealing another person's good name or reputation."
—*Cree-L Kofford*

On June 26, 1858, what I believe to be the largest army in the history of the United States at that time began to enter the Salt Lake Valley. They were sent to overcome a rebellion that was not taking place. They marched in relative silence within a few yards of a church. They went through the town which was deserted because the inhabitants were camped some distance to the west. The army had come to the village of Fairfield, approximately 40 miles south of Salt Lake City, a small farming community in Cedar Valley, where it is estimated that fewer than 200 people lived. The local spiritual leader was John Carson.

Imagine how that small community must have felt. How would you feel if you woke up one morning and found that several thousand soldiers with over 3,000 wagons, 10,000 oxen, and 12,000 mules had moved into your town? Problems immediately began to come up. It is said that Bishop Carson was greatly concerned about the welfare of the members of his congregation and of the community.

To protect the congregation members as much as possible Bishop Carson met with the commander of the fort, who often dined at his inn and with whom he developed a good relationship. The two leaders surveyed the situation and agreed upon drawing a separation line. No army personnel could cross the line and go into the civilian community without the specific approval of their superiors. No congregation member could cross the line and go into the army camp area without specific approval from Bishop Carson. The line on the ground represented an implicit command: "Do not cross this line."

For children who grew up in that environment, a line on the ground had a very special meaning. Children would trace a line on the ground whenever their childish temperament would provoke discord. The kids involved would stand on opposite sides of the line, trying to act as intimidating as possible. "Step over this line and you'll be sorry" was the usual challenge. Reading this story I learned the great value of a line on the ground and the consequences of stepping over it. In the years that have followed, I have come to understand that, figuratively speaking, there are lines traced on the ground by a loving Heavenly Father who seeks to protect us from Lucifer's army.

> "A good name, like good will, is got by many actions and lost by one."
>
> —*Lord Jeffery*

Although many of us may have to deal with several lines of separation in our daily life, I want to talk about just one of them—the line that says, "Honor the good name of the people in your church."

Oscar Kirkham was an excellent Christian in his community. He was respected wherever he was. Frequently in his church's meetings he would ask to say something personal and when allowed he would say something good about someone. Near the end of his life, he spoke briefly at Brigham Young University about the subject "say something good." On the morning Kirkham died, they found a small notebook where he kept his notes. The last two notes read: "Say something good" and "Your good name is safe in our home."[1]

What a blessing it would be if we would follow this counsel and the "good name of each of us were safe in our spiritual house." Have you noticed how easy it is to cross over this line and seek faults in other people? Many times we try to excuse ourselves from the same attitudes we condemn in others. "Mercy for me and justice for everyone else" is a very common attitude. When we deal with the name and reputation of other people, we are dealing with something sacred in the sight of the Lord.

There is a familiar saying: "Never judge another man until you have walked a mile in his shoes." This advice is as good today as it was originally. As Edward Wallis Hoch said, "There is so much good in the worst of us, and so much bad in the best of us, that it behooves any of us to talk about the rest of us."[2]

The principle is not new, neither is it restricted to our time. The book of Psalms contains this warning from the Lord, "Whoever slanders his neighbor in secret, him will I put to silence" (Psalm 101:5).

James, a servant of the Lord, repeated this eternal truth when he said: "Brothers, do not slander one another. Anyone who speaks against his brother or judges him speaks against the law and judges it. When you judge the law, you are not keeping it, but sitting in judgment on it…. But you, who are you to judge your neighbor?" (James 4:11-, 12).

To those who doubt the importance of this biblical orientation, I would like to ask two questions: First, how can you say you love your neighbor when you try to slander his good name and reputation? Second, how can you say you love God when you cannot love your neighbor? Remember the biblical counsel, "Do not let any unwholesome talk come out of your mouths, but only what is helpful for building others up according to their needs, that it may benefit those who listen" (Ephesians 4:29).

Any attempt to justify such behavior brings to mind the powerful words of the Savior found in the book of Matthew: "You brood of vipers, how can you who are evil say anything good? For out of the overflow of the heart the mouth speaks. But I tell you that men will have to give account on the day of judgment for every careless word they have spoken. For by your words you will be acquitted, and by your words you will be condemned" (Matthew 12:34, 36, 37 NIV).

You probably remember the classic children's story of Bambi and all his friends in the forest. You probably remember also that one of Bambi's best friend was a rabbit named Thumper. He was a good rabbit, but he had one problem: he always said bad things about others. One day as Bambi was in the forest learning to walk, he fell down. Thumper couldn't resist the temptation and said, "He doesn't know how to walk very well, does he, Mother?" His mother was upset and said, "What did your father teach you this morning?" Thumper's face fell as he said, "If you can't say something nice, don't say anything at all." That's good advice we all need to follow.

I dream about seeing each church member practicing this principle. When you hear someone say something bad about another person, say, "If you can't say something nice, then don't say anything at all." Or, "We choose not to speak ill at church." Everyone will understand exactly what you are trying to say.

I pray that the Lord will bless us that we may never step over the line, and that we may live in a such way that it can be said, "Your good name is safe in our home." Only then will we be able to write a new page in the history of the church. After all, we are the church, and the mission to establish a positive church in a negative world belongs to each one of us.

---

[1] Marion D. Hanks, foreword to Oscar A. Kirkham, *Say the Good Word*, (Deseret 1958), p. 4.

[2] Hazel Felleman, *The Best Loved Poems of the American People*, (New York: Doubleday, 1936), p. 615.

THIS BOOK COMES FROM MY HEART BECAUSE . . .

I DREAM of a congregation where every participant will feel loved and accepted.

I DREAM of a place where pastors and local church leaders develop their joint ministry with knowledge and wisdom.

I DREAM of a church where leaders are improving their skills, their methods, and their interpersonal relationships toward building Christ's kingdom.

I BELIEVE in a positive church even when the world is becoming increasingly negative.

I BELIEVE in the Holy Spirit's power to help you become more creative in leading your church with Biblical principles and ethics.

I BELIEVE God's church can make a difference for good!

— Jonas Arrais

Jonas Arrais, D.Min., serves as an associate secretary of the Ministerial Association, General Conference of Seventh-day Adventists, with specific responsibility for developing resources for pastors and laity leaders, as well as editor of *Elder's Digest*, a quarterly magazine for local church elders. He has pastored for 25 years, serving the largest churches in Brazil and in the Ministerial Association of the denomination's South America Division. His spouse, Raquel, serves as associate director of the Women's Ministries Department of the General Conference. His son and daughter-in-law, Tiago and Paula, are students at the Theological Seminary at Andrews University, and his younger son, Andre, is in law school. Arrais' ministry has emphasized development of team leadership for pastors and laity elders in creative collaboration for strong church growth.

US$9.9
ISBN 978-1-57847-047-1

SEVENTH-DAY
ADVENTIST CHURCH

9 781578 470471